BEYOND IQ

ALSO BY GARTH SUNDEM

The Geeks' Guide to World Domination
Brain Candy
Brain Trust

SCIENTIFIC TOOLS

FOR TRAINING

PROBLEM SOLVING,

INTUITION,

EMOTIONAL INTELLIGENCE,

CREATIVITY,

AND MORE

BEYOND IQ

Garth Sundem

THREE RIVERS PRESS
New York

Published in the United States by Three Rivers Press, an imprint of the Crown Publishing Group, a division of Random House LLC, a Penguin Random House Company, New York.

www.crownpublishing.com

Three Rivers Press and the Tugboat design are registered trademarks of Random House LLC.

Library of Congress Cataloging-in-Publication Data

Sundem, Garth.
Beyond IQ / Garth Sundem.
p. cm
1. Emotional intelligence. 2. Multiple intelligences. 3. Creative ability. 4. Problem solving. 5. Intuition. I. Title.
BF576.S86 2014
153.9—dc23
2013022757

ISBN 978-0-7704-3596-7
eBook ISBN 978-0-7704-3597-4

Printed in the United States of America

Book design by Elina D. Nudelman
Cover design by Nupoor Gordon
Cover illustration by Hein Nouwens/Shutterstock

10 9 8 7 6 5 4 3 2 1

First Edition

To your brain. It's more than a number.

CONTENTS

In the movie *Pretty Woman,* Richard Gere's character inexpertly drives a friend's Lotus through the Hollywood Hills, grinding the gears, and eventually stops at a red light next to a Dodge Colt. The Lotus has a 345-horsepower, supercharged 3.5-liter V6 engine, which can do 0–100 mph in 9.9 seconds with a top speed of 155 mph. The Colt does not. There's a pretty woman—not the titular character—in the passenger seat of the Colt, and Gere's character cocks an eyebrow in her direction and revs the engine. The light turns green. Gere drops the clutch . . . and the Lotus bucks to a stop as the Colt leaves it in the dust.

That's IQ. You can have all the mental horsepower in the world under your hood, but if you can't drive it, there you are stuck on Hollywood Boulevard amid the smoke of a burning transmission.

In other words, raw intelligence is good: it helps to shape your potential top speed. But there's much, much more that goes into realizing it. This brain-training book for everything but IQ will teach you how to drive your mind—to get the most from what you've got under the hood. Entertaining information will help you understand what these skills are and aren't. Hands-on exercises will boost your wisdom, insight, willpower, problem solving, emotional intelligence, multitasking, and more—all the things that bridge the gap between the intelligence in your head and the results you want in the real world.

Why is it worth focusing on these non-IQ skills? Well, the fact is, while IQ is obviously important to real-world success, it's only part of the picture—and as you'll see in these pages, a far *smaller* part of it than you might think. Haven't you met someone rich and successful who ... didn't seem like the brightest bulb, in the book-learning kind of way? Or, vice versa, someone who's a walking encyclopedia but just can't seem to get ahead in life?

These gaps between IQ and success aren't just dumb (or smart!) luck—they're due to the influence of all these other, often unmeasured, skills. In the coming chapters, you'll see numerous studies and scientists testifying to this fact, but for now, how about just one quick example: According to a study by the former president of the American Psychological Association, Robert Sternberg, and his frequent collaborator, Richard Wagner (no relation to the composer!), *practical* intelligence is actually a far better predictor of job performance than IQ.

And practical intelligence is just one of these non-IQ skills that turns out to matter as much or more than intelligence itself. Emotional intelligence, willpower, creativity, motivation, the ability to perform under pressure—they all make a *huge* difference in our everyday lives. Chances are that with a 115 IQ and all these skills, you'll be happier, more successful, and more fulfilled than a Mensa member who lacks them.

But that's not the only reason to focus on these non-IQ skills. Much as we'd all love to supercharge our IQs, the bad news is you've either got it or you don't. More precisely, something like 80 percent of your

IQ is genetically determined—you can fine-tune it, sure, but to a great extent, the engine you're born with is the one you've got.

And chances are, you've *already* tweaked your IQ as much as you can, even if you don't realize it. How many years of schooling do you have? Twelve? Sixteen? More? Here's a news flash: many of your classes were thinly veiled IQ training sessions, designed to prepare you for standardized tests like the SAT and GRE that measure your IQ. (Really, they do; researchers can use students' SAT scores to predict their IQ to within a few points.) After all that training, how much more room do you imagine your IQ has to grow?

For most of us, the same isn't true of creativity, emotional intelligence, and the rest. Unlike the IQ-type activities most of us practiced in school, the education system spends little time honing these non-IQ skills. (For instance: when was the last time someone explained the mechanics of intuition to you, or told you what science has to say about activating it? Yeah—that's what I thought.) Whereas IQ is a pitcher you've largely filled, your non-IQ brain skills are nearly empty jugs waiting for juice.

So if you're looking to eke out another few points on an IQ test . . . well, you know what to do. Just keep doing the kind of training you've been doing all your life. But if you want to get your brain functioning better in ways that *matter,* stop trying to painfully squeeze another mile or two per hour of top speed out of your already finely-tuned IQ engine. Instead, join me in thinking about how to *maximize the IQ you've already got.* Learn how to drive your mind.

And no, you don't have to take my word for whether this stuff actually works. Every claim and exercise in these pages springs from interviews with some of the country's top brain researchers and studies published in peer-reviewed journals. This is real *science,* people. Here you'll learn what top psychology researchers have to say about cultivating correct intuitions and overbalancing bad experiences with good so that age leads to wisdom. You'll learn to clear clutter from the path to an insightful solution and boost the skills of executive function: willpower, focus, and multitasking. And much more.

Hopefully you'll even enjoy it. That's because this book knows the lesson of the New Year's resolution: a promise to do something you hate will last about as long as your New Year's hangover. Instead, the vast majority of the exercises in these chapters, while remaining scientifically sound, are meant to be fun. You get to dissect the illogical quotes of world leaders, sort ladybugs, solve riddles, role-play as Mac-Gyver, write your own limericks, and combine illustrated elements into Rube Goldberg machines.

That's not to say the exercises in this book are *easy*—if they weren't challenging, they wouldn't do you any good. The moral of the booming field of neuroplasticity is that the more you stretch your brain, the more you can change the patterns of its wiring. And by its nature, a simple path creates a simple brain. Instead, the key to successful thinking and wondering and evaluating is, well, spending time and effort on the brain-bending experience of thinking and wondering and evaluating.

But stretching your mind needn't be horrible and frustrating and boring. Perhaps the most important lesson in this book of lessons is that putting the engine of your mind to hard work can be fun. And while you're having fun putting your brain through its paces, you'll also be pointing the Lotus of your life toward success.

BEYOND IQ

CHAPTER 1

INSIGHT

I was at a thing the other night with a handful of other Boulder, Colorado, authors, ostensibly to talk about writerly stuff but actually to drink beer and swap stories. After a couple of Left Hand Brewing Wake Up Dead Stouts, a defense lawyer turned biographer turned crime writer named Mark told a story about his book in progress, the fifth in a series of crime novels. Set in south Florida, it features hit men with guns, a corpse filled with bullets, and more than a pinch of courtroom drama. Mark talked about how he'd peppered the first two-thirds of the book with clues leading to his meticulously pre-planned conclusion that, in hindsight and in the great tradition of Sir Arthur Conan Doyle, Perry Mason, and Angela Lansbury as amateur detective Jessica Fletcher, could've gone no other way.

Only, it did.

For a couple of weeks, in the back of Mark's mind had been the disappointment that this fifth book was going in the same direction as his first four—not the details, per se, but the mechanism of clue-sprinkling that eventually leads the only place it could lead: to the true killer. You know, the crime-novel thing. One morning he sat down to type as he always does, imagining that in a couple of hours, he'd be two thousand words closer to his scripted finish.

But then—*bang!*—something happened.

The clues came together in his head like the melding of the two panels of a 3D stereogram, only instead of bringing the killer's face into focus (spoiler alert!), the sum of these clues was no killer at all. The hit men found an already-dead body and claimed the crime in order to get paid. Mark described his absolute confidence that the left turn he took meshed with the interconnected web of clues woven into his novel's previous two hundred pages.

He just knew it was right. And in this state of knowing, the words in his head outpaced his typing skills. He found himself attacking the keyboard in a frenzy to crystalize his insight. One day and fifteen thousand words later, Mark had his newest crime novel.

Crime writer Mark's insight is the stuff we all hope for when presented with a tricky problem: a simple, brilliant solution that strikes us seemingly out of the blue. But it seems serendipitous, impossible to re-create.

In fact, while Mark's crime-novel insight was serendipitous in that he didn't necessarily mean to discover clues clicking into new configurations when he sat down at his computer that morning, the insight itself was anything but luck. Without knowing it, he'd entered a state of brain- and knowledge-readiness that made insight nearly inevitable. You can learn to put your brain in the same state.

First, here's why insight can be difficult: It requires a paradoxical mix of experience with openness. Usually, experience leads to set-in-stone ways of doing things. Typically, openness is only present when you're forced by inexperience to remain available in your search for solutions. Experience mixed with openness is a rare cocktail.

Let's unpack this a bit. Insight is the novel connection of far-flung bits of information floating around in your head. And so in order to make connections, you have to have the needed information in your brain already. This is what we think of as experience, or expertise; researchers call it problem-specific knowledge. These chunks of information and know-how form the building blocks of insight. If you're a physicist, your insights come from combining your problem-specific knowledge of physics facts in novel ways; if you're a chef, an insightful dish comes from knowing ingredients and techniques and then melding them together to make something new.

The more problem-specific knowledge you accumulate, the more building blocks you have to use when constructing insight. There's no pill you can take that will instantly implant you with problem-specific knowledge—although chapter 7 on expertise can help you develop it sooner rather than later.

For now, though, we'll focus on the second half of insight: openness. Again, this second step is why insight is dear: it's a rare person who can know the old solutions but keep an open mind to new ones. And it turns out you can make your brain ready and able to link together whatever problem-specific knowledge you have in new, insightful ways. Researchers John Kounios of Drexel University and Mark Jung-Beeman of Northwestern University know how. They pinpointed the brain state of "readiness for insight" by watching subjects' gray matter as they solved remote-association problems—for example: What one word melds with each of the words tank, hill, and secret to make a compound word or common phrase? This kind of remote-association problem gives itself up to insight or analysis, and use of functional magnetic resonance imaging (fMRI) shows that depending on which strategy you use, distinct areas of the brain are at work.

Ready for another paradox? Rather than opening your mind to insight, Kounios and Jung-Beeman show that if you want insight, the best thing you can do is to close it.

A closed mind shows up on an fMRI as activation of the anterior cingulate cortex, your brain's home of inhibiting distraction. It's as if your ACC is a pair of noise-cancelling headphones, and with these headphones in place you're more able to hear your brain's quiet, insightful whispers. But what's even cooler is that fMRI shows that "these brain states are likely linked to distinct types of mental preparation," say Kounios and Jung-Beeman. In other words, by readying your brain, you can increase the chance of insight. The researchers describe this state as the brain shutting its eyes. Here's how to do it:

First, turn off as much outside stimulus as possible so your brain doesn't have to work to inhibit it. Once you've turned off the outside world, turn off the inside world too—release distracting thoughts and the tempting golden apples of the tried-and-true solutions you know from experience. Then, the researchers say, get ready to close your mind even further—prepare to inhibit not only the distracting things that already exist inside and outside your skull but also any new false whispers your brain offers. For example, remember the words tank, hill, and secret? As you look at the word "secret," the whisper of "service" might pop into your mind. Sure, it makes "secret service" but after you discover "hill service" and "service hill" are nonsense, be ready to inhibit the false insight of "service" as surely as you've inhibited background noise and irrelevant thoughts. Shove it quickly and securely into your brain's locked waste vault so that it doesn't compete with other, possibly correct, whispers.

Close your mind.

Assuming you have the problem-specific knowledge, the correct insight is tumbling around in there somewhere. Your job is to silence everything else so that you can hear it. This process of focusing inward, inhibiting irrelevant thoughts, and getting ready to switch to new thinking styles makes you measurably more likely to experience sudden insight, which, in the case of tank, hill, and secret is the word "top," as in tank top, hilltop, and top secret.

Of course, this is unintentionally your mental state when you're sleepy and is why insight tends to strike in bed, in the shower, or while groping for predawn coffee. This generally held opinion of insight-while-sleepy is more than folk wisdom—it's fact. Michigan researchers Mareike Wieth and Rose Zacks showed this by asking 428 undergrads if they considered themselves night owls or early birds, and then having them solve insight problems. Here's the trick: half were tested in the morning and half at night. Students were most insightful when their test time mismatched their preferred time. They did better when they were groggy.

That's not to say you shouldn't sleep. In fact, the opposite is true. A 2004 article in *Nature* showed that when you sleep, you reorganize your thoughts. Science has known that during sleep the brain's hippocampus—the structure responsible for encoding new memories—replays the day's experiences from short-term storage and filters them into the neocortex, where experiences are integrated into what the article calls "preexisting knowledge representations." Insight is the novel connection of knowledge, and sleep knocks knowledge into new configurations. The *Nature* article asked subjects to figure out the next digit in a tricky, coded string of numbers. And it turned out that subjects who were allowed to "sleep on" the problem's difficult instructions were more likely to reach the insightful solution that the second number in each coded string was also the eventual answer. Aha!

Other insight strategies that have earned the stamp of science include being in a good mood and drinking booze. Really: in a 2012 study in the journal *Consciousness and Cognition,* University of Chicago researchers showed that subjects with a blood alcohol content (BAC) of .075 solved more remote-association problems "in less time, and were more likely to perceive their solutions as the result of a sudden insight." In an article in the *Journal of Cognitive Neuroscience,* Jung-Beeman shows that rather than anything independent and magical about joviality and vodka, these two wonder drugs are shortcuts to the same state of brain readiness seen in earlier experiments. You can train yourself or trick yourself into readiness for insight.

This sleepy, unfocused, uncluttered brain state was the serendipitous preparation that Boulder crime writer Mark had as he sat down to type the last third of his novel. Through his past work as a defense lawyer and as a crime novelist, he'd preloaded problem-specific knowledge—he was expert at connecting the events of a crime based on the constellation of its clues. Then when he sat down in the morning at his computer with a mind free of distractions and the false whispers of the way he meant the plot to unfold—bam!—insight crashed into his brain like a football team bursting from the locker room tunnel.

The following exercises will help you learn to hear the whispers of insight. First we'll train the necessary brain state and then we'll work on disentangling problem-specific knowledge from the false assumptions that sometimes accompany experience. Finally, you will be tested.

EXERCISE 1
REMOTE ASSOCIATION

Researchers John Kounios and Mark Jung-Beeman show that mental preparation leads to insight. But what kind of mental preparation? This exercise will help you find this insightful state of mind.

In each of the following sets of words, your task is to find one word that melds with each of the three provided words to make a compound word or common phrase. For example, if the three given words were *pine/crab/juice*, the answer would be *apple* as in *pineapple, crab apple,* and *apple juice.* These are remote-association problems, used by Kounios, Jung-Beeman, and many others to test and train insight. Remember, the trick of insightful solutions isn't necessarily boosting the volume of your insightful whisperings but turning *down* the volume of everything else so that you can hear them. It's as much a task of inhibiting distraction as it is in encouraging insight.

So in each of the following remote-association problems, practice closing your mind in a way that allows insight to be heard over the roar of your usual cognitive background noise. Sit in a quiet place and, after reading the three words, close your eyes, clear your mind, and listen for quiet whispers from the back of your brain. Importantly, when your brain inevitably feeds you incorrect insight, work to quickly inhibit it as powerfully as you inhibit all other distractions. Lock away incorrect insight so that it doesn't intrude on your tabula rasa of readiness.

Over time, this practice should increase your ability to slip seamlessly into a state of mind primed for insight—a state you'll be able to call upon next time you're faced with a real-world problem that requires an "aha!" solution. But don't expect every insightful answer to be immediate! Rather, researchers find that another frequent ingredient of insight is an *incubation period*—sometimes it helps to sleep on it or at least let the problem breathe for a bit. So if an insightful solution resists your mental preparation, rather than immediately checking the back of this book for the answer, let a difficult remote-association problem linger in your brain. You might only get through one or two problems before getting stymied—in that case, move on to another exercise and allow insight to strike when you least expect it. Move into and away from these problems as your insight permits— and then apply the exact same strategy when confronting your real-world problems of insight.

fire/ranger/tropical

carpet/alert/herring

forest/fly/fighter

cane/daddy/plum

friend/flower/scout

duct/worm/video

sense/room/place

Pope/eggs/Arnold

fair/mind/dating

date/duck/fold

cadet/outer/ship

dew/badger/bee

ash/luck/belly

break/food/forward

nuclear/feud/values

collector/duck/fold

car/French/shoe

office/mail/step

circus/around/car

sand/age/mile

catcher/dirty/hot

fly/milk/peanut

tank/notch/secret

thief/cash/larceny

artist/great/route

hammer/line/hunter

blank/gut/mate

list/circuit/cake

master/child/piano

cover/line/wear

beer/pot/laugh

trip/left/goal

blue/light/rocket

man/sonic/star

bus/illness/computer

type/ghost/sky

full/punk/engine

break/black/cake

car/human/drag

liberty/bottom/curve

drunk/line/fruit

buster/bird/wash

fruit/hour/napkin

old/dog/joke

toad/sample/foot

|||||||||||||||||||||||||||||||||||| EXERCISE 2 ||||||||||||||||||||||||||||||||||||
FUNCTIONAL FIXEDNESS

A screwdriver is used to turn screws, not to anchor a tent. A fan is used to cool rooms, not blow leaves. These are examples of functional fixedness—the tendency to get stuck in the rut of an object's name or common use. It's also a special kind of false assumption that frequently needs breaking on the way to insight. In fact, in an experiment with 872 subjects, Temple University researcher Evangelia Chrysikou and her colleagues showed that learning to break functional fixedness led to higher performance on completely unrelated insight problems—breaking this assumption boosts insight in general.

Psychologist Karl Duncker designed the classic problem of functional fixedness—the candle problem—in which you have a candle, matches, and a box of flat thumbtacks, and you must hook the candle to a wall so that when lit it won't drip onto a table below. Of course, the key is releasing your assumption that the box can be used only to hold tacks. Instead, it can also be a shelf, which you tack to the wall. Voilà!

Another more modern psychologist, Harvard researcher Tony McCaffrey, knows how to break this functional fixation. His *generic-parts technique* teaches you to mentally deconstruct an object into its pieces and then ask two questions—(1) can it be broken down further? and (2) does your description imply a use? "Along the way, alternative uses emerge," McCaffrey writes. For example, take a candle. You can divide it into wax and wick. But "wick" still implies a use—better to call it a twelve-inch length of braided cotton. Now you can see that in addition to burning it, you could use the string to tie things together. A study by McCaffrey found that people trained in his generic-parts technique solved 67 percent more insight problems than untrained subjects.

Lack of functional fixedness is also the genius of the TV character MacGyver. For example, in season one, episode four, MacGyver uses a map as a peashooter, a sled, to catch and retrieve a key from the far side of a door, and to patch a hole in a hot-air balloon. Here are further examples from the MacGyver crisis list. In each problem, practice Tony McCaffrey's generic-parts technique to divest the objects of the common uses implied by their names. Without fixed functions, insightful solutions flow.

1. MacGyver needs to power a rowboat. He has a forked branch and a sleeping bag packed in its sack.

2. There's a hole in a rubber fuel line! MacGyver has to repair it with a knife and ballpoint pen.

3. MacGyver needs to move a tub of diamonds from a building's second floor into the trunk of his car. He has a rain gutter and a lampshade.

4. MacGyver has a scarf and a rock. How can he unseat a bad guy from his horse?

5. From fifty yards away, how can MacGyver see the numeric code bad guys type to enter a building, using a newspaper, a magnifying glass, and a watch crystal?

6. MacGyver wants a doorknob to turn in about five minutes, when he's long gone. He has water, two small plastic bags, and fishing line.

7. MacGyver has to plug the slow leaks in an empty car radiator using only water and eggs.

8. MacGyver must use a garden hose and a rake to scale a wall.

9. How can MacGyver use a soccer ball, newspaper, cotton balls, olive oil, and a match to make a flying signal?

10. MacGyver has a bicycle and must shoot a ball bearing with enough speed to generate a spark.

REBUS ROUNDUP

Rebus puzzles use pictures or spatial arrangements to represent words or parts of words. The answers are usually common phrases, as in XQQME translated into "excuse me." James MacGregor and John Cunningham of the University of Victoria, British Columbia, write that, "Solving a rebus requires breaking implicit assumptions of normal reading, similar to the restructuring required in insight." In other words, rebuses force us to draw on problem-specific knowledge—language and reading—in a new, unfamiliar fashion. On the next page, MacGregor offers the rebus puzzles used in a 2009 article for the *Journal of Creative Behavior*. Like the previous exercise, breaking these assumptions of normal language use on the page will help you learn to break similar assumptions when you commute, cook, play chess, or construct.

AGES	BAD Wolf	PUNISH-MENT	league
R.P.I.	amUOUS	XQQME	1 + 345
go stand	A P P E L S A U	person ality	w a t e r
legal legal	big big ignore ignore	s t i u t h s	search and
somewhere — rainbow	a home home	G B E N bush A I T	ro- diamond -ugh
little Large little Large little Large little little lIttle Large	Friend Just Friend	L Y I N G JOB	o r clock c k

INSIGHT FINAL EXAM

In 2003, Mark Jung-Beeman and Edward Bowden tested 144 remote-association problems with 289 Northwestern University undergrads to discover which problems were most difficult. Once you've spent some time training yourself in the art of insight, put your knowledge to the test with the researchers' ten hardest remote-association problems, solved by no more than 3 percent of students in a fifteen-second time limit. Rather than rushing as in the test at Northwestern, try one at a time. Memorize the three terms and then if a solution isn't immediate, let the terms sit. Sleep on it. Come back to them groggy. And see if the training in this section can help insight strike.*

board/blade/back	way/ground/weather
land/hand/house	cast/side/jump
hungry/order/belt	back/step/screen
forward/flush/razor	reading/service/stick
shadow/chart/drop	over/plant/horse

---

* Courtesy of Mark Jung-Beeman, "Normative Data for 144 Compound Remote Association Problems," *Behavior Research Methods, Instruments & Computers* 35(4): 634–39.

CHAPTER 2

PRACTICAL
INTELLIGENCE

What do Brazilian street children and Berkeley housewives have in common? Both are expert mathematicians. A study showed these children carry out complex mental mathematics in order to run successful street businesses, and another showed that Berkeley housewives smoothly compare grocery prices and quantities to make the best per-weight or per-item buying decisions.

This seems like run-of-the-mill IQ until adding another thing that Brazilian street children and Berkeley housewives have in common: neither can do it in the lab. When researchers tested their abilities to perform the same math on paper, neither group could pull it off. Their practical intelligence is born of situation, distinct from and largely independent of general intelligence.

Robert Sternberg, the Yale/Tufts/Oklahoma State researcher peppered throughout this book, told me another anecdote about practical intelligence, which he includes in his excellent book *Practical*

Intelligence in Everyday Life. See, trash collectors in Tallahassee used to pick up bins from customers' backyards. This required parking the truck, walking to the backyard to retrieve a full trash bin, wheeling it to the truck, unloading it, returning the empty bin to the backyard, and then walking back to the truck. This was the method trash managers had taught the collectors, who were mostly high school dropouts and unlikely to have especially high testable IQs. That is, it was the method until one trash collector discovered a more practical solution. Here's a hint: the trash bins were provided by the city of Tallahassee and so were identical. Can you see the solution? It takes practical intelligence but not necessarily IQ to see that if you wheel an empty bin with you during the first trip into the backyard, you can simply trade it for the full one, return to the truck to empty the bin, and then move on to the next house where you trade the newly emptied bin for a full one—repeat as necessary. This simple solution halved the walking time required to turn full backyard bins into empty ones.

When you mash together Brazilian street kids with Berkeley housewives with Tallahassee trash collectors, you end up with a powerful home-brew poison to the traditional conceptualization of IQ: the intelligence we can measure has little to do with the intelligence we express in our lives. Formal studies of IQ and performance agree. For example, Sternberg and his frequent collaborator, Richard Wagner, showed that situational judgment tests (of the kind included in this chapter's exercises) designed to measure practical intelligence are a much better predictor than IQ of job performance in business managers, bank managers, and graduate students.

IQ doesn't lead to success. Practical intelligence does.

This disconnect between intelligence and success is particularly true of two groups. The first is made up of, as Sternberg told me, "people who are walking encyclopedias, but they make a mess of their lives. Getting 100 percent on a written driving test doesn't mean you can drive." People in this group of gifted idiots have much less success than their IQ predicts.

The other group with a disconnect between testable intelligence and success is the flip side of these gifted idiots. Like the Brazilian street kids, Berkeley housewives, and Tallahassee trash collectors, they're all street smarts and no book smarts. Or they're people with strange holes in their IQ—instead of having ye olde consistent level of smarts across the board, they have peaks and valleys of cognitive strengths and weaknesses that add up to average or lower intelligence but allow narrow domains of excellence. These people have more success than their IQ predicts.

In either case, Sternberg shows that practical intelligence grows from something called tacit knowledge—all the unsaid but understood information of culture and situation that allows people to match perfect actions to environments. For example, a student may be able to make an airtight argument in an essay, but without the tacit knowledge that text-message language, full of LMAOs and OMGs, is situationally inappropriate, the student may still earn a low grade. You want this tacit knowledge? Go back even one more step: for the most part, implicit learning creates tacit knowledge (which creates practical intelligence). You don't necessarily mean to acquire this tacit knowledge, you just pick it up in the background of your cognitive life.

We'll get to training tacit knowledge through implicit learning in the exercises that follow, but first let's look at how to best use the practical intelligence you already have. Basically, you can maximize your practical intelligence by ensuring a match between your tacit knowledge and a task. For example, you may have high tacit knowledge of Jamaican patois, but it won't help you interpret this Cockney rhyming slang: "Have a butchers at them knobby biscuits!" Instead, your tacit knowledge needs to match your environment, in this case understanding that "butcher's hook," or "butchers," refers to look and "biscuits and cheese," or "biscuits," refers to knees, making the sentence read, "Have a look at them knobby knees!" Now with your new expertise in Cockney rhyming slang, you can tell the person who budges you in the grocery line to, "Go stick it up your Khyber!"

According to Sternberg, there are two ways to create a match between your existing tacit knowledge and an environment—you can adjust the environment to better mesh with your tacit knowledge, or you can switch environments altogether to cherry-pick one in which you have the tacit knowledge to succeed.

In the first case, shaping your environment to make it more in line with your tacit knowledge might be as simple as pairing yourself on a project with a colleague who has complementary tacit-knowledge skills. Alternatively, you might sit farther away from a frustrating co-worker at a meeting. Imagine how you might shape your environment toward your tacit knowledge strengths.

Then again, if the mechanics of your life allow, it might be easier to simply select a new environment that's a better match for your tacit knowledge. If you know how to survive in a jungle and not in the desert, move to the jungle. If you haven't got the tacit knowledge of family dynamics required to survive Thanksgiving with the in-laws, avoid it like fourteenth-century sailors avoided ships flying the plague banner.

Finally, if you can't adjust your environment or switch it, you'll have to adjust yourself—you'll have to boost your practical intelligence. Again, the string is implicit learning leading to tacit knowledge leading to practical intelligence. Take a butchers at the following exercises to boost this skill.

WASON SELECTION TASK:
EVIDENCE FOR PRACTICAL INTELLIGENCE

This exercise, devised by Peter Wason in 1966, shows that you likely already have practical intelligence. Why? Explaining it here would ruin the result. So complete the following exercises before flipping to the back for answers and discussion.

1. Which of these cards would you need to turn over in order to test the hypothesis that on the other side of every even card is a star?

2. Which cards would you have to turn over to disprove the statement "If a card has a vowel on one side, it has an even number on the other?"

A B 4 7

3. One side shows a person's age and the other shows what they're drinking. Which would you have to turn over to test the idea that if you're drinking alcohol, then you must be over twenty-one?

4. Which of these cards would you have to flip in order to test the statement "What goes up must come down?"

IF, THEN, BECAUSE:
MAKE IMPLICIT LEARNING EXPLICIT

Do you feel out of touch in situations involving work, family, or friends? If so, blame your implicit-learning skills. Implicit learning should pair conditions, actions, and outcomes, leading to tacit knowledge of social cues. But if your implicit learning isn't, well, *implicit,* Robert Sternberg recommends a workaround: make it *explicit.* Train this subconscious learning by making it conscious.

Do it, he says, by stripping situations down to bare-bones frameworks that describe situations, actions, and outcomes. Effectively, a situation described in this way is a crystallized piece of tacit knowledge—a mental Rolodex of these tacit knowledge cards that match a specific environment will increase your practical intelligence in this situation.

Here's how:

Look at the tacit-knowledge template at the end of this exercise. In the IF and AND IF blanks, write the information that sums up the situation. In the THEN blank, list your action in this situation. Finally, list the result of your action in the BECAUSE blank. Now you have situation, action, and outcome. (Note that if your action flopped and you want to avoid similar idiocy in the future, you can list your action as a THEN DON'T.)

Here's how Sternberg describes the experience of a meeting conflict, stripped down to the elements that train tacit knowledge—notice the structure created by the IF, AND IF, THEN, and BECAUSE:

IF <you are in a public forum>

AND IF <the boss says something or does something that you perceive is wrong or inappropriate>

AND IF <the boss does not ask for questions or comments>

THEN <speak directly to the point of contention and do not make evaluative statements about your boss's, staff's, or peers' character or motives>

BECAUSE <this saves the boss from embarrassment and preserves your relationship with him>

It's important to note that this list of proper actions refers to a specific employee and a specific boss. Remember, we're talking about knowledge that *matches a specific environment.* With *your* boss in *your* work environment, speaking to the point of contention might not, in fact, be the best course of action. You need to develop your own tacit knowledge. Again, the trick is learning to consciously observe causes, effects, and reasons in the world around you so that you can form your own conclusions about your specific surroundings. Give it a try and see if you can get the hang of it. Tomorrow, aim to create maybe four or five of these tacit-knowledge cards. Copy and cut out a stack of the templates included here or make your own. When you encounter a sticky situation, think back to crystallize the conditions, actions, and outcome. If you can keep this up for a while, pretty soon you'll have a whole encyclopedia of practical intelligence at your fingertips, which you can flip through when other tough situations arise, either figuratively by thinking back to its contents or literally by flipping through its pages.

TACIT KNOWLEGE TEMPLATE

If _____

_____

And If _____

_____

And If _____

_____

And If _____

_____

Then _____

_____

Because _____

_____

EXERCISE 7
SITUATIONAL JUDGMENT TEST

As you've seen, in order to express practical intelligence, your tacit knowledge needs to match the environment—again, if you know how to live in a jungle but not in a desert, best live in the jungle. However, Sternberg and his colleagues have also shown some crossover in all this know-how. For example, someone who knows how to live in the jungle is more likely than most to also know how to live in the desert. In other words, tacit knowledge and thus practical intelligence can be very domain-specific, but there's also a general component: people tend to have some degree of general street smarts.

You can see this in what are known as *situational judgment tests*

(SJT). Pioneered in the 1920s, these tests present situations along with good and bad actions. By comparing answers to the responses of the top performers, testers—usually HR managers—discover the degree of practical intelligence a job candidate is likely to bring to workplace scenarios. But the thing is, people who score high on SJTs that measure workplace competencies tend to also score high on SJTs measuring life skills or military skills or . . . anything, really.

So your responses to the situation-specific scenarios below aren't as situation-specific as they might seem. Instead, they (generally) measure your overall degree of practical intelligence. And if you want to *improve* your practical intelligence, after answering, ask yourself *why* these actions are the worst and best. Think them through. This process of evaluating tricky experiences not only tests but trains practical intelligence. Although the following situations and answers are modernized, the core dilemmas and solutions are adapted from situational judgment tests by Sternberg and Wagner.

SCENARIO #1:

You're an ambitious new hire as a copywriter at a fast-paced marketing and PR firm. In your first week on the job, you get a Facebook friend request from your boss's boss. You ask around a bit and find that not everyone's been friended—only young, attractive employees like you, not including your boss.

Actions:

A) Quietly accept the friend request.

B) Quietly decline the friend request.

C) Mention the request and your concern to your boss and ask for guidance.

D) Schedule a meeting with your boss's boss to discuss the request and your concerns.

SCENARIO #2:

You're at the park with your young child and a friend who also has a young child. The kids disagree about ownership of a roly-poly bug and quickly come to blows. Your friend grabs her kid from the fray and takes the child to the shade of a nearby tree, where your friend spanks the child for her involvement. All the other parents at the park are horrified.

Actions:

A) Do nothing. A parent is entitled to his or her own form of discipline.

B) Placate watching parents by immediately explaining to your friend that disagreement between kids is normal, and offer to teach your friend mediation techniques.

C) Wait for twenty minutes and then talk to your friend about the appropriateness of her actions.

D) Choose a Dr. Sears parenting book for your book club, of which your friend is a member.

SCENARIO #3:

You're the foreman of a road construction crew working in the hottest days of summer. You were given five weeks to add a lane to a stretch of highway, but then two weeks into the project your boss tells you that due to unexpected circumstances you'll only have another two weeks—four weeks total—to complete the job. You know that if you work efficiently, you'll have no problem finishing in the shortened time, but the next day your crew gripes and groans about the increased work and despite the need to pick up the pace they get even less done than on previous days.

Actions:

A) Explain to your boss that once he set a five-week schedule, it's impossible to cut it to four.

B) Fire and replace the most outspoken slacker on your crew as an example to the rest.

C) Explain to your crew that your head's on the line and you really need their help to make the deadline.

D) Do nothing. Delays in roadwork happen all the time and being behind schedule in this case is perfectly understandable.

SCENARIO #4:

You borrowed your neighbor's lawnmower but when you pulled the starting cord, the mower belched black smoke, caught fire, and incinerated itself leaving naught but a black hunk of metal in the middle of a scorched ring on your lawn. You're certain it wasn't your fault. You're also certain your neighbor will never believe you.

Actions:

A) Explain the situation to your neighbor's wife, hoping she'll intervene on your behalf.

B) Bring your neighbor to the scorched circle and insist he pay for nine square feet of sod to cover the hole.

C) Offer to split the cost of a comparable, new mower.

D) Bring your neighbor a six-pack of Pabst Blue Ribbon as a thank-you for letting you borrow the mower. Wait until he's had at least two before explaining what happened.

SCENARIO #5:

Fresh from an MBA program, you're hired as a mid-level manager in a large tech company. When you start, you're excited to find that you've leaped to a level of the totem pole that takes most employees ten years to reach, and many of the employees below you have been with the company at least five years. Despite being affable and—you hope—competent, your coworkers exclude you from social interactions and you feel the rumblings of discontent and jealousy from all sides.

Actions:

A) Ask for a demotion so that you can work your way up from the bottom like everyone else.

B) Do nothing and hope that your job performance eventually speaks for itself.

C) Confront your detractors and explain that you didn't choose your placement.

D) Defer to peers' judgment to show your respect for their experience.

SCENARIO #6:

You're leading a brainstorming meeting for new product ideas. While writing on a large whiteboard, you turn back to the group and catch a coworker silently mimicking you. The rest of the group seems to be enjoying your coworker's unflattering impression and are horrified to be caught.

Actions:

A) Stop the meeting and ask to be assigned to a different group.

B) Pretend you didn't notice and continue the meeting.

C) Laugh and suggest that everyone must have strange mannerisms, and as an example offer a lighthearted impression of your unkind coworker.

D) Quip that you'd hoped this group would leave middle school in middle school and continue the meeting.

SCENARIO #7:

A coworker with whom you're friendly leaves home-baked treats in the lunchroom every Monday. Because it's free food and packed with sugar everything gets eaten and out of politeness, everyone compliments his baking—but the fact is the treats are never very good. One day, your coworker tells you that he's finally committed to making his dream come true—he's going to quit his job and start a small bakery. He doesn't have a family to support but plans to mortgage his condo to pay for startup.

Actions:

A) Stage an intervention at which you and your coworkers admit that you never really liked the treats and try to persuade the erstwhile baker that his dream is a delusion doomed to failure.

B) Wish your coworker the best. A dream is a dream.

C) Next Monday, buy a plate of treats from the best bakery in town and anonymously set it next to your coworker's underpowered treats in the lunchroom. See what happens.

D) Have a private heart-to-heart with your coworker, explaining your concerns.

SCENARIO #8:

Your friend is convinced that she has the planet's cutest baby. The baby is not cute. The baby is ugly. Sinfully ugly. Your friend coos publicly and constantly about the ugly baby's pulchritude and you're sure it's only a matter of time before someone says something rude.

Actions:

A) Explain to your friend that her baby is ugly.

B) Suggest that perhaps cooing about her beautiful baby in public may make parents with less beautiful children feel bad.

C) Don't touch it with a ten-foot pole. You want no part in this proud mother's eventual realization.

D) When you're around, attempt to make eye contact with quizzical on-lookers to show that you share their realism about the ugly baby, but please, please will they be kind enough to just shut up about it.

SCENARIO #9:

You're a checkout clerk at a grocery store, scanning groceries for a harried mother with three young kids. You can't help but notice that in addition to milk and corn, she's buying nothing but horrendous junk food and two bottles of wine. When her debit card isn't accepted, the mom puts back the milk and corn. Then, when you point out that your automated system won't accept the expired 2-for-1 coupon the mom hopes to use for wine, she gets belligerent and insists you override the system—something that is, in fact, within your power.

Actions:

A) Lie and say that if the customer wants to use the expired coupon, she'll have to talk to the manager.

B) Pointedly suggest that if the wine seems a less good deal without the coupon, perhaps the mother might opt for the milk and corn, instead.

C) Override the system. Get on with your day and let the mother get on with hers.

D) Be friendly and engage the mother in chitchat. Then suggest support services in the community for struggling parents.

EXERCISE 8
NONSENSE AND IMPLICIT LEARNING

The brain wants things to make sense. It wants this so badly that even when presented with nonsense in a Goldilocks range that's not too obviously idiotic, the brain tries to make sense of it. Neuroscience sees the brain's attempts at manufacturing sense as a spike of activity in the anterior cingulate cortex. And it turns out this spike in brain activity in response to nonsense not only helps you interpret the nonsense itself but can help you make sense of the surrounding senseless world. Does that make sense?

"When we channel the feeling [of confusion] into some other proj-ect, it appears to improve some kinds of learning," says UC Santa Bar-bara psychologist Travis Proulx, who explored what happens when you have students read Kafka. In the story Proulx and colleagues used, a country doctor makes a house call to a boy with a toothache only to find the boy has no teeth. Chaos ensues and then lo and behold, the doctor discovers the boy has teeth after all. Fin.

After reading this story, students studied strings of letters, such as "X, M, X, R, T, V." In these strings were subtle patterns—not pat-terns the students could articulate, but when Proulx then showed these students other letter strings, they implicitly realized which fol-lowed the rule. In fact, students who read nonsensical Kafka prior to the letter-string test identified 30 percent more rule-following strings than students who had read a straightforward short story. Confront-ing nonsense improves subsequent implicit learning, the mechanism that trains practical intelligence.

There isn't space here for Kafka, but when you compress sensible nonsense into diamonds, you get Zen koans. To prime your implicit learning as in the Proulx experiment, try wrestling with some of the following nonsense koans, drawn from the great tradition of Zen Bud-dhism. Within this nonsense lies sense—struggling to find it in these koans will help prime the implicit learning that allows you to find hid-den sense in your life.

1. A monk was asked to discard everything. "But I have nothing," he exclaimed. "Discard that, too!" ordered his master.

2. Bokuju was asked, "We have to dress and eat every day. How can we escape from that?" Bokuju answered, "We dress, we eat." "I do not understand," persisted the questioner. "Then put on your food and eat your dress!" replied Bokuju.

3. Hokoji, a Confucian, asked haiku poet Basho, "Who is he who does not keep company with any living thing?" Said Basho, "I will answer that when you swallow the Hsi Ch'iang River in one draught."

4. A monk asked Master Joshu, "Does a dog have Buddha-nature?" Joshu replied, "Mu."

5. Huìnéng asked Hui Ming, "Without thinking of good or evil, show me your original face before your mother and father were born."

6. If you meet the Buddha on the road, kill him.

7. A student asked Master Yun-Men, "Not even a thought has arisen; is there still a sin or not?" Master replied, "Mount Sumeru!"

8. A monk asked Zhaozhou, "What is the meaning of the ancestral teacher's coming from the west?" Zhaozhou said, "The cypress tree in front of the hall."

IMPLICIT LEARNING TEST

Psychologists Barbara Knowlton and Larry Squire show that your declarative memory—the conscious memory that you can articulate—isn't necessarily an asset on the path to practical intelligence. When they tested the implicit learning of amnesiacs against that of subjects with functioning memories, they found little difference.

Here, you'll use an exercise similar to theirs to test your own implicit learning. First, look at the box of strange bugs on the following page, focusing on each bug carefully for about 5 seconds. Give yourself a little break and then take another pass through this box of bugs, evaluating each in turn. Stop! Do it now before continuing to read these instructions.

OK, these bugs are "dingbits." They are dingbits because they share 7, 8, or all 9 features characteristic of a dingbit. Now, without referring back to the training bugs, look at the 96 test bugs on page 31. Are they dingbits? Do they have at least 7 dingbit features? Circle the dingbits and cross out the non-dingbits. There are about half as many dingbits as non-dingbits.

But rather than depending on declarative memory, intelligence, and analysis to discover the similarity and make the call, try to use your implicit learning of the dingbit category. Which animals *feel* like dingbits to you? Check your answers and the discussion at the end of this book. If you like, work half the test, train your implicit learning via the nonsense strategy above, and then return to the second half of the test to check for improvement.

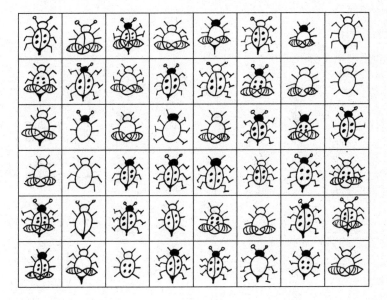

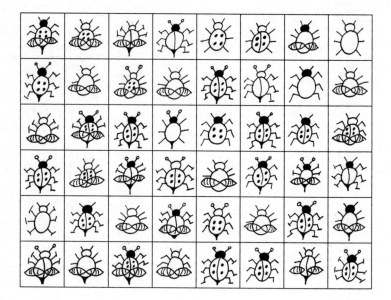

NEUROBIOLOGY OF THE AGING BRAIN

Yale researcher Elena Grigorenko shows that people with an "even," or average, cognitive profile can end up shackled to mediocrity. "Once you're in the middle, you're in the middle on everything," she says. Instead, people who slip or are pushed from this cognitive middle are forced to develop practical intelligence. Failure is common, but those who compensate for nonstandard general intelligence with unique practical intelligence "can blow right past the middle," Grigorenko says. For example, people with the risk factor of low or especially high IQ can and sometimes do compensate with creativity. "If they have a problem in one domain, they are often able to super-develop the other ones. And most of our interesting people, the people we think about and write about are unbound by the middle. Anybody who contributed to human history does not see the middle. Those cases in many ways are the ones who move us forward. These are the Nelson Mandelas of the world," Grigorenko says.

CHAPTER 3

PROBLEM SOLVING

Problem solving is what happens when many of this book's skills align. Insight, creativity, practical intelligence, wisdom, perhaps expertise—all can contribute to a solution. That is, if you line them up right. That's what this chapter's about: how do you set up a problem and choose a solving strategy so that your other skills can knock it down? It's trickier than it sounds.

For example, between 2010 and 2012 Metropolitan State College of Denver worked on the problem of a name change. See, the word "college" translates as "high school" in Spanish and connotes a technical school in French, and so partly to boost recruitment of students for whom English is a second language and partly to highlight its continuing education and graduate programs, the college wanted to change its name to university. The problem seemed easy: what's the best wording for a new name that includes the word "university" instead of "college"?

There's a way you go about a higher education name change. First, the administrators conducted a survey and found that the name Denver State University came out on top, favored by 36 percent of faculty, staff, and students. But the existing University of Denver didn't appreciate the closeness of the new name, and the Colorado state legislature promised to veto the school's attempt at becoming DSU. So MSCD went back to the drawing board and came up with the seemingly easy switcho-changeo of university for college, making Metropolitan State University of Denver.

They checked to see if MSUD.edu was available. It was. Then the college hired a firm to make sure the acronym didn't duplicate that of any out-of-state institutions. Now moving smoothly, it turned out MSUD was unique in academia. The new name coasted through the Colorado state legislature and on April 18, 2012, Colorado governor John Hickenlooper signed bill SB12-148, making the name change official.

"But no one thought to Google it," said university spokesperson Cathy Lucas, doing damage control on Colorado Public Radio. It was damage control because, unfortunately, when you Google "MSUD," the first full page consists of information and parent forums for Maple Syrup Urinary Disease, a serious pediatric health condition in which the body can't break down certain proteins and instead excretes them in urine. It can be fatal. And due to an extremely active parent community that posts about the disease, even a search engine optimization blitz by the college-now-university would be unlikely to unseat the insidious condition. Confounding its name with a pediatric disease perhaps wasn't the path to prestige the university imagined.

Richard Mayer, professor at the University of California–Santa Barbara, author of the book *Thinking, Problem Solving, Cognition,* and one of the most prolific researchers in the field of educational psychology knows how you and I can avoid similar mistakes. "Sometimes it's useful to see a problem in abstract—represent it as its salient conditions and then strip these conditions of false assumptions," Mayer says. This generates what researchers call an initial state and helps you see a problem's constraints. On the far side of a problem is the goal state. And to get there, you'll have to perform some sort of workable operation. And in the language of problem solving, that's it: initial state, constraints, operations, and goal state.

It's tempting to focus on the operations needed to transform the initial state to the goal state. I mean, that's the solution! But Mayer says that the most striking feature of people who successfully solve real-world problems is the time they spend studying the initial state and the constraints—the extra time they spend clarifying the problem.

Take the job of Agriculture Minister of the former Soviet Union. Way back in 1983—when the USSR still existed—researcher James Voss posed subjects the following problem: "Suppose you are the Minister of Agriculture for the Soviet Union. Crop productivity has been too low for the past several years. What would you do to increase crop production?" Description of the initial state says nothing about the weather or the Soviet political system. The constraints say nothing about the availability of arable land. Operations are open-ended. And how much must production increase in order to reach the goal state—1 percent? 25 percent? 200 percent? When Voss gave the problem to Soviet policy experts, political science undergrads, and chemistry professors, he saw something important in the way they went about solving it: The Soviet policy experts spent 24 percent of their solution time elaborating the initial state and constraints, whereas the poly-sci undergrads and chemistry professors spent only 1 percent of their time getting the facts straight.

In part, this was due to Soviet experts' prior knowledge about the Soviet Union—they knew enough to ask about arable land and the Soviet political and social systems; they knew enough to poke and prod the problem's constraints. Of course, the Soviet experts' solutions were generally more reasonable than the other groups' solutions. Understand the problem and a solution will follow.

OK, so how exactly do you go about clarifying those initial states and constraints?

For a classic example of this process in action, Richard Mayer points to a problem first posed by Karl Duncker in 1945. "The classic tumor problem works like this," Mayer says, "you're a doctor and your patient has an inoperable malignant tumor in the middle of his abdomen. Radiation will kill the tumor, but radiation strong enough to do the job also destroys any healthy tissue it passes through on the way to the tumor. Without operating, how can you use radiation to kill the tumor without killing any healthy tissue?"

Take a minute. Or two. Can you solve this problem? When I chatted with Mayer, I certainly couldn't. Like many problems, the solution depends on correctly conceptualizing it from the start. First explore inside the problem and try to isolate the smallest possible point where you seem hopelessly stuck—work to abstract the initial state and the constraints.

In the tumor problem, Mayer says that people usually pass through a couple of common ideas before narrowing in on the real crux. First, they think to toughen up the healthy tissue and then blast radiation through the whole thing at an intensity that kills the tumor but not the strengthened healthy tissue. "But this violates one of the problem's constraints," says Mayer, namely the fact that radiation strong enough to kill the tumor necessarily kills healthy tissue it touches. "There are a few other versions of that," Mayer says, "and then people generally start to think about how to avoid contact with the tissue—maybe they think to remove the tumor and then zap it, or insert a tube and shoot the radiation through it." But both require an operation. "And eventually problem solvers come to understand that the radiation has to be weak in the healthy tissue and stronger in the tumor," Mayer says.

Bingo! This is the small box in which the real problem rests: how can the radiation be weak in the tissue and strong in the tumor? Restating the problem in this way focuses problem-solving power on the most difficult part. Assuming a solution exists, it will exist in this box. This is the problem's true initial state.

Now that you've got the initial state nailed down, it's time to figure out the problem's true constraints. Are you making any false assumptions that are keeping you from finding a solution? Now that you've drawn a small box, widen it to make sure you include all possibilities.

Mayer suggests separating constraints from false assumptions by trying to "wiggle" your visualization. In your visualization of the tumor problem, do the constraints allow you to wiggle from a male to a female patient? Sure, but it doesn't really matter, so move on to the next. Could the patient be sitting or standing? Of course, but that doesn't seem relevant either. Do you visualize a single, gun-like ray delivering the radiation? If so, maybe it's worth releasing this assumption. Wiggle your visualization to imagine other possibilities. "Examining their actual knowledge about a situation and comparing it to their assumptions tends to lead people to recognize that you could have many rays, all firing at varying intensities," says Mayer.

With this initial state and constraints, the operation that leads to the goal state is fairly simple: low-intensity radiation must be delivered by many coordinated rays all firing into the tumor from different angles. No one ray will be strong enough to kill the healthy tissue it passes through, but the head-on collision of all the radiation at the point of the tumor will be enough to fry it.

And that brings us back to the Metropolitan State University of Denver. Their administrators isolated the initial state—how could they replace "college" with "university" in a way that made the new name unique? But they failed to separate constraints from false assumptions, namely failing to recognize and revise the assumption that the new name would compete only with acronyms within higher education.

Now you have the tools to handle the first two steps in solving life's ill-defined problems: examining initial states and constraints. But if even after elucidating the problem's conditions the solution doesn't smack you in the head, you'll need to move on to thinking about which solving strategies can help you arrive at the answer—the domain of operations. The following exercises will help you do it.

EXERCISE 10
PROBLEM-SOLVING OPERATIONS: RANDOM, DEPTH-FIRST, BREADTH-FIRST, AND MEANS-ENDS ANALYSIS SEARCH

There are a number of ways humans go about solving problems on paper and in the real world, and knowing the names of these techniques and how they work can help you match the problems of your life with the best solving strategy. So let's look at random, depth-first, breadth-first, and means-ends analysis searches.

This sounds a little tricky and technical until you imagine problem solving as a journey through a maze—the initial state is your starting point, the goal state is the finish, and the constraints are the rules: you can't jump walls. Simple! And keeping these three conditions simple allows us to work on the fourth: the operation you use to draw the path.

On the first maze that follows, try a *random search*. Really: don't think. Don't look ahead. Don't look back. Put your pencil at the start and just go. Hit a dead end? Try it again from the start, randomly. OK, OK, this obviously doesn't work very well and in this case is more a thought experiment than a solution strategy.

But there are situations in which random search is, in fact, the

best operation! The ideal operation depends on what researchers call a problem's *search space*. With a simple search space—if there were very few turns in this maze—it might actually be easier to solve it randomly than to donate brainpower to the planning and execution of a more nuanced operation. Likewise, if it took nanoseconds to test each path, it might be faster to randomly try them all rather than thinking about *how* to try them. So: *Random search is best when trying paths is quick, easy, painless, and likely to lead to a solution more quickly than extensive planning.* For example, imagine the power is out in your house at night—if your goal state is the bathroom across the hall from your bedroom, random search should do it. But if your goal state is the leftover carrot cake in the fridge downstairs, the more complex search space may require more than random search: it may require a flashlight. (This extra layer is referred to as "subgoaling," and we'll look at it more later.)

On the next maze, do a *depth-first* search. Still without looking ahead, follow one path to its absolute dead end, and if that end is not the goal state, back up to the most recent junction and try the path not previously chosen, following it to its end. If that isn't the goal state either, continue retreating to each previous junction and trying the next path. On a paper maze, your pencil shows which branches of the search space you've exhausted, and possibilities are likely few enough to remain manageable. But in life and in many other puzzles, like chess, a depth-first search quickly requires massive memory. So: *a depth-first search is usually best when possibilities are few or when you don't have enough information to nix unlikely branches of the decision space.* (In the language of problem solving, a rule that allows you to chop out a portion of the search space is called a *heuristic*; adding heuristics to depth-first searches can be a powerful strategy.)

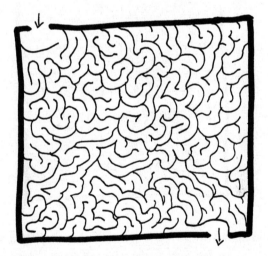

Try again, this time with a *breadth-first* search. Go to the first junction. Look down the left path. Does it eventually branch again? If so, it remains a possibility: draw a small arrow pointing down that left path. Now go back to check the right path. Does *it* eventually branch? If so, it also remains a possibility: draw a similar arrow pointing down this right path. Now go back and check each of those branches in turn to see if it branches again. If not, make an *X* instead of an arrow—this path is closed. A depth-first search allows you to get lucky, to serendipitously find a path that snakes all the way from initial state to goal state. But is it the best path? In a maze it doesn't really matter. But in life, *a breadth-first search keeps all options in play until they are absolutely nixed. Instead of following one thread to its lucky or unlucky end, a breadth-first search explores all paths at once a little at a time and so may lead to multiple answers, some better than others.*

Finally, try a *means-ends analysis.* This solution strategy explores the differences between the initial state and the goal state and tries to chip away at each difference until none remain. It's how water would trickle down through a jumble of rocks, always flowing toward its goal even if the flow is along a slope of only one degree. In a maze, the difference between the initial state and the goal state is the difference between *x* and *y* coordinates, so at every turn, take the branch that heads most toward the goal. Unfortunately, in mazes, as in life, it's frequently necessary to move away from your goal so that you can eventually move toward it—without the ability to flow upward, water may get stuck in a cupped boulder and never reach the ground.

Here's where we get to *subgoals*. Your subgoals may initially appear to be parallel to or even headed away from the goal state, but in combination they'll get you there—and unlike the convoluted path from initial state to goal state, the path to each subgoal can be straightforward (or at least much less twisty!). Chimps set subgoals, too. In 1927 German psychologist Wolfgang Köhler placed his prize chimp, Sultan, below a bunch of bananas with two sticks just too short to reach them. Sultan quickly saw the subgoal—he needed a tool long enough to reach the bananas and so hooked the two short sticks together.

In a maze, subgoals may be bottlenecks through which the path obviously must pass. Or you can create subgoals by working backward—starting at the goal state and retreating to the first ambiguous turn provides a subgoal for use when switching to working the maze from the initial state.

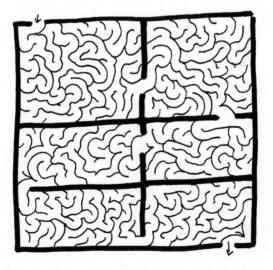

In a maze, there's really only one constraint: don't jump the walls. But in life, subgoaling may look more like applying one constraint at a time. For example, when picking a baby name, you might narrow the problem space by boy names, and then by family names, and then by names that won't get the poor child teased in middle school. Each subgoal is a bottleneck through which the solution must pass.

These are the most common human solution strategies—random search, depth-first search (likely with heuristics), breadth-first search, and means-ends analysis (likely with subgoals). If you have the time, it's worth taking another pass through these strategies with new mazes (try the ones on KrazyDad.com). The idea here is not so much to solve the mazes, of course, as it is to practice putting these strategies into action and thus get them to stick in your head.

MATCH: INITIAL STATE TO OPERATIONS

Now that you've previewed the most common human solution strategies on paper, it's time to put them to use in the labyrinth of life. Following are examples of situations best solved by the four operations you learned in the previous exercise. Match the situation to the best solving strategy. Then in the space provided, add your own examples of problems best solved by each search strategy.

OPERATIONS

Random search: Without planning or reflecting, try for a quick solution.

Depth-first search: Once you start down a path, follow it to its end. Not the solution? Retreat and try again.

Breadth-first search: Dip a toe into each possible path to a solution, nixing only the ones that prove impossible.

Means-ends analysis: Chip away at every factor that divides initial state from goal state, perhaps pointing at subgoals along the way.

Situations:

1. You are a man dressing formally and need to put on underwear, pants, undershirt, shirt, socks, belt, cufflinks, tie, jacket, etc.

2. Looking at a map, there are many routes you can use to commute from home to work. Which is the best?

3. You need a pair of black socks in a hurry. There are many white along with equally many black socks in a drawer.

4. You are at work. You are hungry. There's a cash-only vending machine. You have a card but no cash. There's an ATM downstairs.

EXERCISE 12
FALSE ASSUMPTIONS

As we've seen, arriving at a clear-eyed understanding of a problem's initial state can be the key to reaching a solution. And researchers Afia Ahmed and John Patrick of Cardiff University know how to do it. In 2006, they presented subjects with two problems, including the following, known as the Unseen Walker Problem:

> On a busy Friday afternoon, a man walked several miles across London from Westminster to Knightsbridge without seeing anybody or being seen by anybody. The day was clear and bright. He had perfect eyesight and he looked where he was going. He did not travel by any method of transport other than by foot. London was thronged with people yet not one of them saw him. How?

Then Ahmed and Patrick asked subjects to talk through their answers. Only 42 percent of subjects solved the problem, and in unsuccessful solvers the researchers found something in common—what they called a "constraint that could block participants from reaching the correct answer." We'll call it a false assumption. What do you incorrectly assume about the Unseen Walker Problem? Well, if you assume the walker is traveling aboveground, as did the unsuccessful solvers, you were almost certainly stumped. But what if he travels belowground in the sewers? Aha!

Then Ahmed and Patrick ran the experiment again, only this time they taught their participants to be on the lookout for these false assumptions. The training had two parts: first, they used an example to make participants aware of the blocking effects of assumptions. You've had an example already in the Unseen Walker Problem. And the second part of their training helped participants identify and overcome these assumptions in new problems.

The trick is learning to compare a problem to *your interpretation* of the problem (in these pages or in life!). For example, compare the following problem and interpretation from the ingenious book *Lateral Thinking Puzzles* by Paul Sloan and used by Ahmed and Patrick:

Problem: Archie and Ben were professional golfers and keen rivals. One day during a game, they had each scored 30 when Ben hit a bad shot. Archie immediately added 10 to his own score. Archie then hit a good shot and he had won the game. Why?

Interpretation: Two friends were playing golf, they were both on 30 points, then one reached 40 points and won.

Now ask yourself how the interpretation fails to match the problem—what does the interpretation assume that the puzzle doesn't necessarily provide? Must they be playing golf? Of course not! And releasing that assumption should allow an insightful solution:

they're playing tennis, in which Archie's score goes from 30 to 40 with Ben's bad shot and then Archie wins the game on his next good shot.

After Ahmed and Patrick's training, subjects' solution rate for the Unseen Walker Problem jumped from 42 percent to just over 80 percent. On a second problem in which an airplane's bomb doors open but no bombs fall, initially only 8 percent saw the solution—but after training, 50 percent of subjects saw that the airplane must be flying upside down. In both cases, the researchers verified that whenever participants remained unsuccessful, a pesky, unidentified assumption was to blame.

Now that you've received this training, let's see how you do. Solving each of the following problems requires releasing a common false assumption. As in the examples earlier in the exercise, practice comparing your interpretation to the problem, looking for that sneaky assumption that blocks the solution. If needed, write or draw your interpretation (or both!) and then go through the problem, clause-by-clause, checking to see which elements are defined by the problem and which are figments of your interpretation. As Ahmed and Patrick's work demonstrates, as you learn to eliminate these false assumptions your solution rate should rise.

1. FEISTY KINDERGARTENERS

There are four feisty kindergarteners on a standard elementary school playground. How can a playground aide arrange them so that they are all exactly the same distance apart?

2. BATTLESHIP

Move 4 stars to form 5 straight rows of 4 "ships" each.

3. CAR TROUBLE
It's a dark and stormy night and you're driving down the street when you notice three people at a bus stop: an old woman who needs a doctor ASAP, your best friend, and the date of your dreams. You can only fit one other person in your car. What should you do?

4. HOUSEHOLD PETS
There are 114 million households in the United States. The average household has 1.8 pets. If you multiply together the number of pets in each household, approximately what number do you get?

5. COCONUT GROVE
In 1942, Boston's Coconut Grove nightclub caught fire. Patrons rushed the doors but despite the fact they were unlocked, the doors couldn't be opened and 492 people were killed. The incident led to one important safety modification. What was this modification?

6. NOT *THAT* PRISONER'S DILEMMA
A prisoner is locked in a tower with a window high above the ground. He has a rope long enough to reach halfway down. He cuts the rope in half, ties the two ends together and lowers himself safely to the ground. How is this possible?

7. CUT THE CARD
How can you cut a hole in a standard playing card large enough to put your head through?

8. SOCKS IN A DRAWER
White socks and black socks are in a drawer, with five white socks for every four black socks. How many socks must you pull from the drawer in order to ensure a pair of the same color?

9. JANE AND JANET

Jane and Janet are sisters born five minutes apart to the same parents and yet they are not twins. How is this so?

10. MATCHSTICK MATH

How can you move one matchstick to make the following equation true?

$$V - VIII = III$$

|||||||||||||||||||||||||||||||||||||| EXERCISE 13 ||||||||||||||||||||||||||||||||||||||||||
SLIDING TILE PUZZLES

You've seen sliding tile puzzles: with one open square, you must slide the other square tiles to put numbers in order or complete a picture. Psychologists use sliding tile puzzles to test and train three components of problem solving: subgoaling, chunking, and planning. First, subgoals provide manageable waypoints on the path to a seemingly insurmountable solution. For example, completing the final row and column of a 4x4 puzzle effectively makes it into a 3x3 puzzle. Second, "chunking" moves into learned sequences can help you reach these subgoals, for example automating the moves needed to switch a tile with one directly above it. Finally and most important, solving a sliding tile puzzle requires planning—because there are 181,440 possible board states in the 3x3 puzzle and about 653 billion states in the 4x4 puzzle, it's pretty unlikely you'll stumble blindly to an answer. Instead, you have to plan how you will sometimes move away from your goal so that you can move toward it. Researchers at the University of Nottingham showed that when solving the 3x3 puzzle, subjects who immediately started pushing tiles used an average 49.8 more moves than people who planned. And the preplanning group saved an average of 150 seconds per puzzle.

These skills of subgoaling, chunking, and planning ahead are major components of solving many real-world problems. Here you'll practice these skills by making your own sliding tile puzzles. After looking at the following example, copy and cut out the number tiles and arrange numbers 1 through 8 into a randomized 3x3 grid with a tile missing (as in the example). Now your goal is to slide these tiles within the grid to put the numbers in order (again, as in the example). Spend some time planning: what's a reasonable subgoal? What useful "chunked" sequences of moves can you memorize? Once you get comfortable with the 3x3 puzzle, try 4x4 or even—*gasp!*—5x5.

Note that these sliding tile puzzles are either "even" or "odd"—half of the starting positions allow you to put all numbers in order and half of the starting positions will end with the final two numbers frustratingly reversed. Consider either position an answer!

6	4	
3	2	7
1	5	8

→

1	2	3
4	5	6
7	8	

1	2	3	4	5
6	7	8	9	10
11	12	13	14	15
16	17	18	19	20
21	22	23	24	

RED ADAIR

Think the abstract problems in this chapter have no real-world purpose? Think again. Until his death at age eighty-nine in 2004, Red Adair was a stalwart and legend in the tight-knit community of oil-well fire-fighters. In 1961, when a break in a natural gas pipe in the Algerian desert sent up a flame deemed the Devil's Cigarette Lighter, which John Glenn saw from space and melted the desert sand into glass, Adair drove a bulldozer with a boom up to the blaze and dropped eight hundred pounds of explosives on the fire while his lieutenants "Boots" Hansen and "Coots" Matthews sprayed him with water to keep him from vaporizing in the heat. The explosion sucked all the oxygen away from the fire, extinguishing it and allowing Red and his team to cap the pipe.

In 1991, the US government sent Adair to Kuwait to put out the if-I-can't-have-them-nobody-will fires of Saddam Hussein's retreating army. At seventy-five years old, his slightly less cowboy MO was to pipe in seawater and dowse fires with a massive volume of water. But one well was too far from the sea. There was enough fire retardant foam on hand to squelch the fire, but Adair knew that the hoses were too small—the fire would laugh at the flow of retardant each one could spray. Sound familiar? Instead of firing a single, ill-fated stream on the blaze, Adair stationed firefighters all around the blaze, each with a small hose. When Red gave the signal, they all opened up and put out the fire in minutes—just like the tumor problem earlier in this chapter.

CHAPTER 4

CREATIVITY

University of California–San Bernardino researcher James Kaufman knows the recipe for creativity. It's equal parts intrinsic motivation, experience, and something he calls low personal inhibition.

Intrinsic motivation is pretty self-explanatory, but beware the danger of "replacing intrinsic motivation and a natural curiosity with external rewards," says Kaufman. If a parent wants a child to become a creative pianist, the parent should encourage interest in the piano but not incentivize this interest with ice cream. Creativity blooms in fields you're drawn to, not in fields into which you're pushed.

Experience might sound like an odd ingredient to creativity—we like to believe that creativity springs from nothingness like Venus emerging on the half shell. But in fact, it comes from extensive practice. Kaufman's research has shown that creative people are hard workers with background knowledge and expertise in their creative domains. "It's the 'learn the rules so you can break them' approach," he says.

Finally, to intrinsic motivation and experience, truly creative people add low personal inhibition, which Kaufman explains with the following example: "Usually when you walk into a hotel lobby, you don't start shouting profanity. This isn't because you never have the fleeting urge to shout profanity, but because you inhibit this urge," he says. Which is not to say that all creative people shout profanity in hotel lobbies—but they tend to feel less personally constrained by societal norms.

Each ingredient sounds straightforward, but when you look at the mix, you can see why so few people successfully cook up creativity. It requires motivation independent of external reward, years of painstaking preparation in the field, and the rare pairing of conscientiousness with abandon. Also, while these three factors open the possibility of creativity, expressing it also takes perseverance. For example, Dean Keith Simonton of UC Davis found that the nineteenth-century scientists who wrote the most-cited papers also wrote the least-cited papers. In other words, even with motivation, experience, and low personal inhibition, not everything a creative person creates will be creative (even an industrious and talented woodchuck will not always succeed in chucking wood). Instead, contribution is the hit-or-miss product of somewhat random chance—the more scientific papers or sonatas or sonnets a person writes, the greater chance that one or more will be especially creative.

So the basic ingredients of lifelong creativity are a tricky brew.

Luckily, there are some mind-sets and strategies that can boost the short-term expression of creativity. Learning these can help you next time you're presented with a problem requiring "out-of-the-box" thinking. Following are some of science's best tricks for boosting creativity.

INSPIRED, DIVERGENT THINKING

Consider the Mad Hatter's classic riddle, as infuriatingly written by Lewis Carroll: "Why is a raven like a writing desk?" Alice gives up, but you should not. Instead you can train your brain to come up with creative solutions to questions that, like this one, require divergent thinking.

Whereas *convergent* thinking describes narrowing down possibilities until converging on the one correct answer, *divergent* thinking is its opposite—you start with given conditions and create many possibilities, such as how a raven could possibly be like a writing desk, or the possible uses of a drinking straw. And while ravens and writing desks might be a bit silly, there are plenty of real-world conundrums that are rewarded by this ability to brainstorm many possible solutions and draw unexpected conclusions.

First consider what Andreas Fink of the Austrian Institute of Psychology saw when he watched subjects' brains with fMRI when he asked them to come up with creative, alternative uses for everyday objects such as bricks or paper clips. First Fink had participants do it cold. Then after an appropriate interval he had them reflect on their ideas and try it again. Finally, he presented participants with others' ideas and had them complete the task a third and final time.

Here's the punch line: unlike the first two conditions, being confronted with others' creative ideas sparked creativity in his participants—they came up with more, creative uses for umbrellas and tennis balls and the like. Fink and colleagues saw this jump in creativity as increased activity in areas of the brain responsible for memory, attention, and language processing—exactly paralleling the three ingredients of creativity: experience, intrinsic motivation, and low personal inhibition. Perhaps this "idea sharing," as Fink calls it, could be the key to historical pockets of creativity, like Florence of the

Medicis or the Harlem Renaissance or China's Tang dynasty. In any case, the point here is that *experiencing* creative ideas will make you more creative.

So before diving into the Carroll-esque divergent-thinking riddles below, prime your own creativity by considering some creative answers to Carroll's first, famous riddle—a raven is like a writing desk because: (A) The notes for which they are noted are not noted for being musical notes (Sam Loyd, 1914); (B) Poe wrote on both (Loyd); (C) There is a *b* in "both" and an *n* in "neither" (Aldous Huxley, 1928); (D) They both come with inky quills (anonymous); (E) Neither is made of cheese (no applause, please).

1. How is a butterfly like a sunbonnet?

2. How is a platypus like a pencil sharpener?

3. How is a pumpkin like a propeller?

4. How is an emu like a kazoo?

5. How is a rabbit like a coffee cup?

6. How is a bicycle like an electric mixer?

7. How is a birdhouse like a bowling ball?

8. How is an old dog like a paper mill?

THE BOOK OF NONSENSE

Stanford's Margaret Boden says that "unpredictability is often said to be the essence of creativity. But unpredictability is not enough. At the heart of creativity lie constraints. Random processes alone can produce only first-time curiosities and not radical surprises." This is why my answer to the raven-and-writing-desk riddle in the previous exercise is so much less interesting than the first four: the fact that neither is made of cheese is unpredictable but sidesteps the problem's constraints. Instead, a truly creative solution is more than mere novelty or unpredictability. "Constraints and unpredictability, familiarity and surprise, are somehow combined in original thinking," Boden writes.

As an example of constraints that allow creativity, Boden mentions limericks. "Limericks cannot be written in blank verse, but some 'space' for choice exists," she writes. So let's train our creativity within constraints by completing some famous limericks, drawn from the classic 1846 *Book of Nonsense* by English poet and artist Edward Lear. In each of the below, the final three lines of the limerick are missing. Complete them according to the rules of rhyme, as well as your own taste and moral compass. Once you're done, you can search online for Lear's completions. The first is from Lear and demonstrates the limerick rhyme scheme.

> *There was an Old Man with a beard,*
> *Who said, "It is just as I feared!"*
> *Two Owls and a Hen,*
> *four Larks and a Wren,*
> *Have all built their nests in my beard.*

There was an Old Person whose habits,
Induced him to feed upon rabbits;

There was a Young Lady whose eyes,
Were unique as to color and size;

There was an Old Man who supposed,
That the street door was partially closed;

There was an Old Person of Buda,
Whose conduct grew ruder and ruder;

There was an Old Man with a gong,
Who bumped at it all day long;

There was a Young Lady of Norway,
Who casually sat on a doorway;

There was a Young Person of Crete,
Whose toilette was far from complete;

There was a Young Lady whose bonnet,
Came untied when the birds sat upon it;

EXERCISE 16
FIGURE COMPLETION

A frequent task in creativity tests is figure completion. The subject is given a few lines and is asked to incorporate them into a creative drawing. Drawings are then scored for originality and things like expressiveness, movement, humor, and richness. As with many exercises in this book, this task doesn't just test the skill in question but can help to train it as well. For example, when North West University professor Esmé van Rensburg found unusually low creativity scores among South African children, she designed a training intervention to combat these low scores and included practice with figure completion of the kind seen on the test. Here, practice and thus train your creativity within constraints by incorporating the given lines into creative drawings of your own.

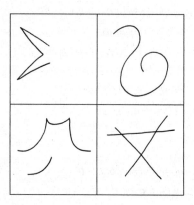

EMBODIED COGNITION

How you act influences how you think—this is what's known in psychology as *embodied cognition* and has been quite in vogue since about 2008. For example, researchers found that holding a pencil in the teeth to force a frown hinders subjects' comprehension of pleasant sentences, that holding a warm drink predisposes subjects to like people, and that subjects like the look of Chinese writing better when they pull characters toward themselves than when they push the same characters away. Similarly, researchers Eli Finkel and Paul Eastwick showed that in speed-dating sessions in which one gender sits while the other rotates, daters who sit and are approached are more liked than daters who rotate and must do the approaching.

Here's what this has to do with creativity: researchers at Cornell, New York University, University of Michigan, and Singapore University noticed that many cultures use the same metaphors to describe creativity. Namely, they found that English, Hebrew, Korean, and Chinese cultures use the expressions "put two and two together," "think on one hand and then the other," and "think outside the box." Could this intercultural similarity be more than coincidence? Could these metaphors, in fact, be serendipitously expressing the cognitive roots of creativity?

To test this idea, researchers had subjects act out these metaphors. One experiment had people sit inside or outside of a 5x5 box while brainstorming what to name ambiguous objects. Another had subjects gesture with one hand and then the other (or with the same hand again) while imagining uses for a university building. In these trials and a couple more, subjects who *embodied* metaphors for creativity were more creative than subjects who did not (really!).

So to train your creativity, you'll do the same. Of course, in order to notice the creativity boost of acting out a metaphor, you'll need a task on which to test yourself. Here we'll use a version of the venerable Cartoons Test, developed by researcher Yvonne Treadwell in 1970. Much like you would for the *New Yorker* magazine caption contest, unleash your creative brain to caption the following cartoons, which Treadwell showed to be a clean test of creativity.

First perform one of the following embodied-cognition tasks and then caption a cartoon (which are drawn from the works of nineteenth-century poet and cartoonist Edward Lear). Continue alternating tasks and cartoons. Does it get easier? Admittedly, this seems silly. But creativity can certainly be silly, and creative action—no matter if it's silly—stimulates creative thought.

If it's impractical for you to sit beside a cardboard box when confronting problems of creativity at work or at home, don't despair: a follow-up study showed you don't actually have to *do* these things— you don't, in fact, have to embody the cognition. For instance, researchers found that watching a Second Life avatar sit outside a box or point with one hand and then the other put subjects in the frame of mind to outperform others on creativity tasks. Do these cues count as disembodied embodied cognition? Are they subconscious reminders to think creatively? Whatever the reason, the point is that even *imagined* versions of embodied metaphors are proven to work. So once you get in the habit of using these cues, you should be able to draw on their power without making your coworkers think you've gone loopy.

EMBODIED COGNITION TASKS:

1. Sit on the floor next to a cardboard box.

2. Walk in the pattern of a rectangle and then intentionally break this pattern to wander aimlessly.

3. Gesture at an object with one hand. And then do the same with the other hand.

4. Put two and two together: shuffle together two stacks of cards.

CARTOONS TEST:

CREATIVITY GRAB BAG

Here, for your pleasure and edification, are five of science's most entertaining creativity-boosting mini-tips:

1. **REM sleep:** A 2009 study in the *Proceedings of the National
Academy of Sciences* shows that REM sleep and not necessarily
quiet rest or non-REM sleep increases creativity. (Note that this
is distinct from the slightly groggy state that produces insight.)
Researcher Denise Cai and her colleagues found that REM
sleep "enhanced the formation of associative networks and the
integration of unassociated information." In other words, REM
sleep allowed subjects to consolidate information in networks that
allowed creative connections.

2. **Think or don't think about death:** Awareness of our own
eventual demise makes us seek social connection. Researcher
Clay Routledge and his colleagues reminded subjects about their
impending death and then had them write proposals to promote
a rock concert. How creative were subjects' proposals? Well, if
subjects thought the proceeds of the concert would benefit charity,
their proposals were much more creative than proposals from
subjects who thought they'd pocket the proceeds themselves. If
your creativity would benefit a group, spend a minute to reconnect
with the idea of your own mortality.

3. **Manipulate trust:** A person's level of trust enhances group
creativity but stifles personal creativity. (And conversely, a little
distrust can make you more powerfully, individually creative.) This
is because the feeling of connectedness can also make you bound
by group norms—it ups Kaufman's factor of personal inhibition.
Distrust of others makes creative, mad scientists.

4. Dance: Researchers Elizabeth Hutton and Shyam Sundar of Penn State University used the videogame Dance Dance Revolution to show that pairing either low excitement and a bad mood or high excitement and a good mood enhances creativity.

5. Embrace multiculturalism: A team from France, Singapore, and the United States showed that multicultural experience fosters creativity, writing that, "Creativity is facilitated in contexts that deemphasize the need for firm answers." A multicultural society shows that one culture's rules and customs may not be the only way to exist.

EXERCISE 19
RUBE GOLDBERG MACHINE DESIGN CHALLENGE

Every year the Rube Goldberg Society and Purdue University host a contest in which engineering geeks from around the country compete to accomplish simple tasks in convoluted ways. For example, on March 26, 2011, a team from the University of Wisconsin–Stout won the competition with its machine that successfully watered a plant ... in 244 steps. Along the way, the machine told the story of a deserted Louisiana estate whose ghosts come to life with the full moon.

Now you'll apply similar skills of creativity and inefficiency to solve the problems of past years' Rube Goldberg Machine Contests. Here's how:

- Copy and then cut out the Rube Goldberg design elements that follow.

- Arrange these elements into "machines" that in combination solve the given problems in the specified number of steps.

• Assume the following rules: (1) Elements can be arranged however you like and will stand anywhere without additional support; (2) String can be cut; (3) Animals will attempt to approach any presented food; (4) Any force (applied in the correct direction) will activate the subsequent element irrespective of size or presumed mass; (5) You may not use any additional elements of your own design; (6) Use your creativity to weave a "storyline" of movement through these elements, however farfetched.

Copy and cut out these Rube Goldberg machine elements:

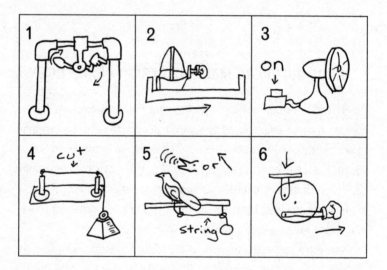

RUBE GOLDBERG PROBLEMS

Start by pushing the car down element number 14, and insert 5 steps before dispensing hand sanitizer.

Start by lighting the fuse of the rocket in element number 13, and insert 8 steps before pushing down the toaster handle.

Start by turning on the fan in element number 3, and insert 7 steps before smashing this orange to juice it.

Start by pushing the pin-laden paper airplane down the ramp in element number 16, and insert 5 steps before turning the crank to sharpen the pencil.

Start by cutting the string that holds the balloon in element number 11, and insert 9 steps before turning off the alarm clock.

Start by clapping your hands to startle the bird in element number 5, and insert as many steps as possible before squeezing toothpaste onto the brush.

CREATIVITY, INNOVATION, AND SOCIETY

We say *we want creativity, but we don't. Not really. For example, teachers routinely cite promoting creativity as one of their top classroom goals but then have been shown to overwhelmingly dislike students who exhibit curiosity and creative thinking. CEOs do likewise, citing creativity as one of the most important employee characteristics—but creative people lag behind their less creative peers in promotions. And it's not just* creative *people that CEOs and teachers dislike—when presented with menus of ideas, teachers and CEOs consistently prefer mundane ideas over their creative counterparts.*

James Kaufman says part of this seeming hypocrisy is that teachers, CEOs, and our culture as a whole mislabels creativity as their goal when what they really want is the innovation that can come from it.

"You can have all the creativity you want in your head, but it's the ability to follow through that links creativity with innovation," Kaufman says. Creativity is thinking thoughts that have never been thought before. Innovation includes the practical intelligence that can help others see the benefit of this thinking.

CHAPTER 5

INTUITION

Intuition is knowing without knowing how you know—a facial expression triggers the intuition of a lie; the way a racehorse flicks its tail makes bettors intuit a winner; or the pattern of a fire and the layout of a house make a firefighter intuit that there is an infant trapped in an upstairs room. (These three examples have been extensively studied.)

Trying to define intuition would make a Greek polemicist tear out any remaining hair. In fact, it took a fairly hefty helping of research by Fernand Gobet and Philippe Chassy to even understand what most people mean by the term. Their 2008 meta-analysis found that most definitions of intuition include "rapid perception, lack of awareness of the processes engaged, concomitant presence of emotions and holistic understanding of the problem situation." You know, that knowing-without-knowing thing.

And so it seems like magic.

Actually, it's anything but.

Instead, intuition is a very specific kind of subconscious learning. As you move through your day, certain conditions follow other conditions and over time when you see the first condition, you start to intuit the arrival of the second. This subconscious pairing of cause with effect allows you to know things without knowing how you know them. But Eugene Sadler-Smith, professor of organizational behavior at the Surrey Business School in the UK, points out the big danger of intuition: "Intuition is a hypothesis—it's a gamble, not a guarantee."

The good news is that you can learn to evaluate and adjust the way you form intuitions, thereby training the good ones while weeding out the bad. Intuition researchers call environments that train correct intuitions "kind" and ones that train incorrect intuitions "wicked." A kind training environment requires an obvious if-then link between the cause and its effect. For example, the unambiguous and exacting feedback of rain helps you pair it with the black clouds that preceded it. Next time you see black clouds, you intuit rain—cause is paired with effect. In a wicked training environment, feedback can be inconsistent, irrelevant, or unexacting, leading you to intuit connections when none exist, such as a black cat in the road leading to bad luck.

Or take the phenomenon of gluten intolerance. Does a child only sometimes turn green after munching wheat (inconsistent feedback)? Might her greenness have been caused instead by eating those chocolate-covered raisins she found between the couch cushions (irrelevant feedback)? And is the child in fact looking green and not just sulking because I—er, I mean "someone"—said she couldn't put the dog on the trampoline (ambiguous, unexacting feedback)? Thus may a certain, unnamed parent's belief that her child is gluten-intolerant be born of wickedness, leading to the unnecessary purchase of $6 loaves of crumbly bread.

You can learn to counteract this wickedness. The psychologist Carl Jung called intuition "perception via the unconscious," but by making intuition conscious you can evaluate the accuracy of existing intuitions and ensure that future intuitions are kindly trained.

Here's how:

First, flip the direction in which you train intuition. Generally we notice an effect (a sick child) and go looking for a cause (gluten?). But in a wicked training environment, working backward from an effect allows your intuition to pair it with any cherry-picked cause—is looking green due to gluten or to sleeping next to a guinea pig? Instead, test intuition by starting with a cause and monitoring the consistency of its supposed effect. When the child eats gluten, how often does she then feel sick? When you see a black cat, how often is it followed by bad luck? Do black clouds always lead to rain? Don't let your subconscious give undue weight to the rare times cause leads to effect while disregarding the many times the cause is present and the effect fails to show.

The next step is ensuring that feedback is relevant. Maybe you've found that the feedback in this case is consistent—every time your child eats gluten, she feels sick, but then at the same time, she's constantly snacking on delicious nuggets harvested from between the couch cushions, making gluten an also-ran to the power of foraged chocolate-covered raisins. So after proving a consistent link between cause and effect, ask yourself if there could be any other cause. Is the pairing relevant or is it coincidental to some other, true cause?

And the final step in training correct intuition is to ensure the effect is actually an effect—is the child really feeling green or is she just tired and obstinate? Feeling sick is inexact feedback. Barfing would be exacting.

Don't give up on intuition—there's no need to completely flip your decision-making process to analysis—but instead, by creating consistent, relevant, exacting feedback (by turning a wicked training environment into a kind one!) you ensure the voice of intuition is an angel and not a devil on your shoulder.

Of course, you can also accidentally turn a kind learning environment wicked.

One way to do this is to manufacture the link between cause and effect. For example, in his book *Educating Intuition,* psychologist Robin Hogarth tells the story of his friend, Anna, a waitress. When the restaurant gets busy Anna can't pay attention to all customers and so prioritizes her time based on the customers she intuits will leave the best tips. She prioritizes well-dressed customers, gives them the most attention, and, sure enough, they leave the highest tips! But isn't it equally likely that her attention and perhaps not their clothes is what's responsible for the high tips? Rather than correctly intuiting the link between dress and tip, Anna creates that link.

I fell into the same trap while playing the Kingdoms of Camelot iPhone game. It seems as if the cities of more powerful opponents should be plump with more resources—and so when I go in to take away these resources by force, I send more supply carts than I might when invading a weaker city. But sending more supply carts allows me to carry out more plundered supplies, and so I create the intuition of a link between mighty cities and rich resources when in fact I might be getting more resources from these cities simply because I'm sending more carts.

In any case: beware of your own influence in creating links between cause and effect.

Likewise, Eugene Sadler-Smith warns against what he calls "the tyranny of small numbers." Maybe a cause has always led to an effect ... but you've only seen cause and effect once. In that case, you can't tell if your intuition is based on the norm or on an outlier. To combat this tyranny, Sadler-Smith recommends practice, and lots of it. He shows that HR managers need to train their hiring intuition across many candidate interviews. Your ability to predict rain depends on the smell of thick air before twenty storms. And a child who turns green after eating a bagel one day doesn't necessarily have a gluten allergy.

"We use intuition in situations in which we have to make complex, often social judgments, frequently without all the information needed for certainty," says Sadler-Smith. "I've never met anyone who can will an intuition into happening, but then when it does, you have to ask, 'How does it fit with my experience? Have I met similar situations before?' Our intuitive mind tells us something and we have to be able to recognize it, acknowledge it, and then perhaps transform it until it's useful."

The following exercises will teach you how to do just that.

RETRAIN ATTENTION, RETRAIN INTUITION

People with social anxiety disorder suffer from faulty intuition—they unfairly pair faces with the expectation of meanness. Researchers have shown this intuition disorder is at least in part the fault of attention—people with social anxiety disorder give too much attention to negative faces. Maybe you see fifty positive and ten negative faces on the way home from work, but if you give the negative faces six times the attention you give the positive ones, you learn to intuit nasty intentions in the social world around you. The same is true of alcoholics and arachnophobes—they give too much attention to the pleasure of drinking or the danger of spiders.

Researchers at Florida State University used a therapy called cognitive bias modification (CBM) to retrain this faulty intuition for people with social anxiety. Basically, they presented a happy face alongside a nasty face and had participants report a letter flashed in place of the happy face. This forced two things: first, subjects had to swing attention quickly to the happy face and second, perhaps even more important, subjects learned to inhibit their urge to fixate on the negative face. At the end of training, 72 percent of subjects no longer met the criteria for the diagnosis of social anxiety disorder, compared to 11 percent of patients who completed a sham version of the training. Four months later, the cured subjects remained cured.

This shows that with practice, you can retrain your faulty intuitions. Sure enough, CBM has been used successfully to treat depression (the intuition that everything sucks) and general anxiety (the intuition that everything is out to get you).

Here's a version of CBM that should slightly brighten your view of humanity, though you can certainly imagine retraining intuition about food preference (pictures of healthy versus unhealthy snacks), or fear of dogs (pictures of dangerous Dobermans versus cuddly puppies), or a fashion sense stuck in the 1990s (modern versus yesteryear styles).

Photocopy and then cut out the slips below. In each, there is a positive and a negative face. Stack these slips faceup. With one hand, flip over the top slip to reveal the next. Then as quickly as you can, use your other hand to slap the happy face. Pull this slip and slap the happy face on the next one. As you flip and slap slips, the attention you pay to positive faces will gently overwhelm the attention you pay to negative ones. With practice, you should start to intuit a happier world.

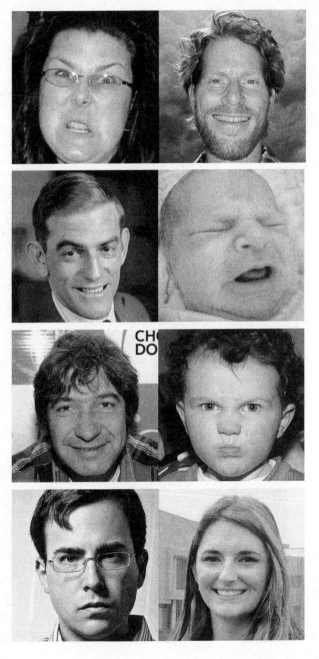

KIND AND WICKED INTUITION

The intuition researcher Robin Hogarth calls environments that train correct intuition "kind" and environments that train incorrect intuition "wicked." When a cause leads consistently and unambiguously to a definite effect, the kind training environment automatically creates correct intuitions. When feedback is absent, ambiguous, inconsistent, influenced by your actions, or based on few experiences instead of many, the resulting wicked training environment can create incorrect intuition.

The point of this exercise is to learn to recognize the difference, first on paper and then in your life. Label each of the situations below kind or wicked, and then for the wicked training environments, list what you would change in order to make them kind and thus able to train correct intuitions. Flip to the answers section of this book for discussion. Then once you've got the hang of it, search your life for similar patterns—every day this week, list one intuition you have and analyze how this intuition was trained. Was the training environment wicked or kind? Could you affect this environment in the future? And is the intuition helpful or hurtful?

1. You're an emergency room physician. Late one Saturday night a forty-two-year-old patient presents with shortness of breath and general lethargy. A CT scan shows a slight shadow in the patient's left lung and your intuition whispers about the possibility of lung cancer. You refer the patient to a specialist for follow-up.

2. When you and your spouse were first dating, you found an unfamiliar shirt in the laundry that, in fact, belonged to your spouse's ex. Oops. Now you've been married six years and lo and behold here is another unfamiliar shirt in the laundry. Your intuition screams affair.

3. You're an HR manager with ten years' experience evaluating job candidates. Sure, you look at résumés and references, but what really matters is how a candidate comes off in the room—what's your intuitive evaluation of a candidate's worth to the company? Once you make your hiring decisions, the candidates who become employees become part of the nameless, faceless corporation and you never hear how they performed in their jobs.

4. You're the same HR manager as in the previous example, but after a six-month training period and then eighteen months on the job, you get the performance evaluations of the employees you interviewed.

5. You're the same HR manager as in the previous two examples, only this time employees receive no training before starting the job. They go straight from your office to work, and then two years later you get their performance evaluations.

6. You're a new hire and during your first week on the job you try to engage a coworker in lunchroom conversation—but your coworker is distant and terse. You intuit that she doesn't like you.

EXERCISE 22
ARTIFICIAL GRAMMAR

Researchers at UCLA and Harvard write that, "Having good intuition about 'what fits' and 'what's coming next' is essential to achieving one's goals .... Life is filled with scripts and recipes that have natural sequences and humans routinely take advantage of the predictability of these sequences to coordinate their thought and behavior."

This exercise uses a tool called artificial grammar to train your ability to hear and appreciate this intuition of what fits. Training and testing are below, and then explanation is included in the answers section at the end of this book.

First spend three seconds looking at each string of letters in the training box. Hold each string in mind long enough that you can copy it from memory onto a piece of paper. If you forget the string while copying it from memory, look at it for another three seconds and try again. Repeat that look-and-writing-down process for each of these strings before continuing to the test.

Training Box:

WWZ	NNZ	WSWZ	NPNZ
NNPZ		NPPNZ	WWSNZ
WSSWZ		WSWSNZ	NPPNPZ
WWSNPZ		WSSWSNZ	WWSPPNZ
NNPSPPNZ		WSSWSNPZ	NPNPSPPNZ

Now here's the test: The strings you saw in the training box were all constructed according to a specific, complex rule. In fact, the rule is so complex that it's not worth trying to figure out. Really, don't try—you'll just end up having some kind of infarction. Instead, look at the letter strings in the following test box and use your gut, hunches, and what might feel like guessing to decide which follow the rule and which do not—circle the "legal" ones and cross out the "illegal" ones. There are sixteen of each. Then flip to the back of this book for answers and discussion.

WSWZ	NPSNZ	WSWPZ	NPNPZ
NWNPZ	WNSWZ	NPPNZ	NPNWZ

WSSWZ	NPNPZ	WNWSNZ
WWSNPZ	WNSWZ	NSPSNZ
WWSNWZ	NNPSNZ	WWSPPNZ
WSSWSNZ	NWPSPPNZ	WSWSNZ
WSSWPNZ	WWSPPWZ	NSWSPNPZ
NNPSPPNZ	NPPNPSNZ	NPNSSNPZ
WSWSPNPZ	NPPNWSNZ	SWSPNPZ
NPNPSNPZ	NNPSPPNPZ	WWSPPNPZ

A HAND IN INTUITION

There was a famous early-twentieth-century New York City physician renowned for his ability to intuitively diagnose typhoid. It sounds like a kind learning environment—you have a patient with symptoms that are or are not definitively typhoid (consistent, unambiguous feedback). But by one action, the physician made this a wicked training environment: he felt patients' tongues with his bare hands as part of his examination, thus very literally having a hand in making a link that might not otherwise have existed. It wasn't so much a patient's symptoms that predicted typhoid as the physician's disease-laden fingers scrabbling around in a patient's mouth.

CHAPTER 6

YOUR BRAIN ON TECHNOLOGY

In April 2012, Mark-Andre Duc sat in a hospital in the southern Swiss city of Sion, controlling the movements of a foot-tall robot at Switzerland's Federal Institute of Technology, about sixty miles away. Alone, the feat is far from newsworthy—on average, the Earth is about 150 million miles from Mars and human controllers manage to drive the rover *Curiosity*. But Mark-Andre Duc was different from NASA rover pilots in one important way: he's paralyzed. Unable to move his fingers or legs, Mark-Andre Duc drove the robot with his mind. Wearing a cap of electrodes, he imagined lifting a left finger to turn the robot left and imagined moving a right finger to turn the robot right. A computer linked to his "thinking cap" decoded his brain's slight electrical signals and relayed the commands to the remote robot.

Then a month later, a woman who preferred to remain anonymous and so was known as "S3" sat in a chair facing a robotic arm. Attached to the surface of the motor cortex of S3's brain was a bean-sized implant with ninety-six thin electrodes that read the patterns of her brain activation. Though paralyzed fifteen years earlier, S3 controlled the robotic arm with her thoughts, using it to lift a cup of hot coffee to her lips and take a sip.

Just as Mark-Andre Duc and S3 used their brains to control technology, you can use technology to control your brain. For example, the American Psychological Association recommends the use of electroconvulsive therapy to treat severe depression. A practice known as deep brain stimulation inserts electrodes that act like pacemakers to control the tremors of Parkinson's disease, the fixations of obsessive-compulsive disorder, the pain of a phantom limb, or even to improve spatial memory—helping subjects learn to accurately navigate virtual mazes.

If you're going to run 800 milliamps and a couple hundred watts through your brain as in electroshock therapy, or insert metal wires deep beneath your skull as in deep brain stimulation, best leave it to trained professionals, preferably with steady hands and multiple PhDs.

But there's a third modern form of firing electricity into your brain that you can do yourself this afternoon! Powered by a nine-volt battery, transcranial direct current stimulation, or tDCS, is relatively safe, and in addition to the obvious recreational value of running current through your gray matter, an explosion in recent research shows that this little bit of electricity can go a long way toward boosting a number of brain functions.

That's because your neurons generally sit around waiting for electricity to reach a critical threshold, at which point—*pop!*—they fire, propagating current along their lengths. Transcranial direct current stimulation increases the baseline electricity that neurons feel, and so it takes less additional electricity to make neurons in the area fire. If neurons were little guns, adding the gentle electric current of tDCS would be like changing out a twenty-pound spring for a hair trigger.

Speaking of guns and triggers, some of the best evidence for the usefulness of tDCS comes from tests by the US Defense Advanced Research Projects Agency (DARPA), which studied the use of tDCS to train snipers. Training took place in a virtual environment called DARWARS and used videogames to train recruits in things like the rules of engagement, cross-cultural communication, and how to blast the heck out of a never-ending swarm of virtual attackers. DARPA being DARPA, it apparently seemed too mundane to simply present recruits with an onslaught of bloodthirsty ambushers when they could do the same thing to recruits while firing electricity through their brains!

Electricity has to make a circuit and so recruits wore a moistened anode (which shoots electrons) on their right temple and a cathode (which sucks electrons) on their left upper arm. The exact version of DARWARS played by electrified recruits had them survey a scene for danger—"a shadow cast by a rooftop sniper, or an improvised explosive device behind a rubbish bin," writes Douglas Fox in the journal *Nature*. Recruits had to recognize the threat and neutralize it before it neutralized them. And with electricity coursing through their brains, they did it more than twice as well as non-electric (acoustic?) recruits. In threat recognition, speed, and marksmanship, tDCS made recruits better. Do a quick Google search for tDCS, and you'll see more than a dozen studies showing similar gains in learning or performance.

Because tDCS runs current from a "plus" wire to a "minus" wire, not only can you boost the function of a brain region, you can simultaneously lower it in another. For example, the right anterior temporal lobe is implicated in sudden insight, but is undermined by the naysaying left anterior temporal lobe. Researchers hooked up tDCS to amp the right and blunt the left and saw a resultant rise in aha thinking.

And for the common pairing of schizophrenia and depression, tDCS can increase mood in the left dorsolateral prefrontal cortex while decreasing activity (and thus hallucinations) in the temporal cortex.

So what is this tDCS wundermachine? You're probably picturing a pricey MRI tube full of whirring fans and blinking lights—and, in fact, a well-known cousin of tDCS, transcranial magnetic stimulation, lives up to that expectation, costing about $50,000 for a rig. But speaking at a neurotechnology conference, Harvard's Eric Wasserman said, "Half the people in this room could build [a tDCS machine] with parts from RadioShack." The device is simple: a nine-volt battery is connected with wires to large, flat sponges that are moistened and then applied to the head.

Oh, and maybe you're wondering if it's safe. Believe it or not, before attaching electrified sponges to human heads, researchers have wondered the same thing. The Department of Neurophysiology at Georg-August University in Germany zaps as many patients with tDCS as anyone, to treat conditions including migraines, tinnitus, and post-stroke complications, as well as healthy subjects for the purpose of science. And they asked 102 of these patients about their side effects. As expected, 70.6 percent of them felt mild tingling during tDCS and 35.3 percent reported feeling mildly fatigued afterward. A few reported headache (11.8 percent), nausea (2.9 percent), and insomnia (0.98 percent), but this was within the expected range of people who might have felt these complications even without tDCS. A study at the City College of New York found that the most harmful side effect was rare instances of skin irritation at the site of the electrodes, and used animal models to explore the upper limits of tDCS current. Let's just say it's unwise to exceed 149.2 amps per square millimeter of brain surface. However, even if you could suck all the amps instantaneously from a nine-volt battery in one great shock (which you can't), you wouldn't hit this threshold. Just keep it to a single nine-volt and to twenty minutes per pop and you should be good to go—you know, in an at-your-own risk, only-if-you-dare kind of way.

Seriously: use at your own risk. While results to date seem to indicate that tDCS is safe, you are messing with your brain here. And because this is a new field, studies on the effects of long-term or repeated use are still lacking. I'm not telling you that it's a good idea to try this. Still think that turning your brain into a DIY electric guinea pig sounds fun? If so, the following exercise describes the results of successful tDCS studies and how to approximate them at home.

EXERCISE 23
DIY TDCS

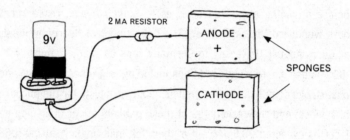

This diagram shows how to construct the basic tDCS machine, although many variations exist (or you can order one for about $350 from the company Mind Alive). Now the question is where to stick the sponges. Pick your desired result from the list of studies below, and then apply the anode sponge as shown in the numbered diagram that follows, and place the cathode sponge on your upper arm.

1. At MIT, tDCS of the primary motor cortex helped subjects learn a fine motor skills task.
2. At Harvard, tDCS of the dorsolateral prefrontal cortex increased subjects' performance on a working-memory task.

3. A tDCS study at the University of Zurich found that stimulation of the right prefrontal cortex made subjects more forgiving.

4. Researchers in Boston and São Paulo, Brazil, collaborated on a study that found tDCS on the left dorsolateral prefrontal cortex increases executive function, making subjects less impulsive and less risk-seeking.

5. DARPA's tDCS marksmanship training, explained earlier.

6. University of Sydney study mentioned earlier, which increased insight by tDCS of the anterior temporal lobe.

7. Many studies show benefits of tDCS of motor regions affected by stroke (e.g., Nair et al, 2008; Hummel et al, 2006; Hesse et al, 2007). Search online for images of "motor cortex map" and apply anode to affected area.

8. The NIH Behavioral Neurology Unit found increased verbal fluency after tDCS of the left prefrontal cortex.

9. A number of studies use tDCS to treat depression, most commonly anodal stimulation of the left dorsolateral prefrontal cortex.

10. A Harvard clinical trial of *cathodal* tDCS of epileptic brain areas led to 64.3 percent reduction in epileptic discharges. Apply cathode to affected area.

11. A Harvard study found increased memory for musical pitch with tDCS of the left supramarginal gyrus.

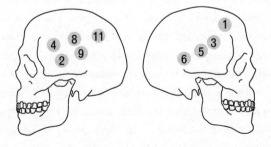

DIY tDCS was simply too delicious to pass up. I have to admit it wasn't my first experience with off-label use of electrical apparatuses on my body—a couple of years ago I hooked my wife's TENS machine to an especially tight lower back and ended up twitching on the floor like a mean drunk hit with a police Taser. So it wasn't completely without trepidation that I affixed the sticky, electrified pads to my skull.

In a test meant to simulate DARWARS, my kids would sneak around the house trying to surprise and pummel me with foam lightsabers while I targeted them with a Nerf N-Strike Maverick REV-6 blaster.

When the machine went live, the anode tingled. I'm not sure what I expected, but instead of the revelatory shouting of the voice of surety, it was more like I'd ball-gagged the voices of distraction. Whatever was happening, it was definitely something. I felt clear. And then irrespective of how clear I felt, I was brutally beaten by foam lightsabers and the experiment came to an end. Let's just say it wasn't exactly lab conditions.

THE END OF MEMORY

Direct current isn't the only way technology affects the brain. Computer games are now played for an average of 6.3 minutes at a sitting, with smartphone apps played only 2.2 minutes at a stint—in other words, we're using games to plug even the smallest holes in our cognitive downtime. The bad news is that—as researchers at San Francisco State showed in a study using maze-running rats—cognitive downtime lets learning take hold. "Almost certainly, downtime lets the brain go over experiences it's had, solidify them and turn them into permanent long-term memories," says study author Loren Frank.

But maybe we don't need memory anymore—not when we have Google. A study published in the July 2011 issue of the journal Science *finally, definitively, found that Google allows us to forget things. Specifically (and this is cool), the study found that when we're sure we'll have access to information in the future, we forget the information but boost our ability to find it. "Instead of remembering 'ends' we're remembering 'means,'" says Betsy Sparrow, the study's lead author.*

CHAPTER 7

EXPERTISE

Play along, now: you're white and it's your move. What do you do? Well, if you thought to slide over your corner rook to threaten the black queen, congratulations—consider yourself a chess expert! But in this case, the expert move is not the *best* move. Here's what happens: black ignores your rook's threat and instead moves bishop to threaten your queen. You *stay on target, stay on target* and capture the black queen. And feisty black retaliates by squishing your attacking rook with a black rook of its own. You still have no way to save your white queen. So by playing the obvious, expert move, you lose your white rook and queen, while black loses only its queen.

Expertise is great, except when it's not. Here's the trap: when presented with a familiar situation, experts may act according to the kneejerk of their experience while overlooking unfamiliar best solutions.

To learn more about expertise in general and this trap in particular, I spoke with Paul Feltovich, research scientist at Florida's Institute for Human and Machine Cognition and renowned expert on expertise. "In any kind of cognitive activity you have two kinds of things going on," Feltovich says. "You have intelligence, but there's also learning and skill and knowledge based on practice. The more the second develops, the less important the first becomes." You can see this in chess players: among young players, the most intelligent do best. But as chess players age and gain expertise, intelligence ceases to matter—once chess players reach age thirty, hours of experience and not IQ mark the best players.

"Even more importantly," says Feltovich, "we've shown that with enough practice and hard work, you can actually change the neurophysiology of the brain. For example, practice can encourage the brain to grow greater myelin coating on neurons. Thus our behaviors become literally hard-wired. Developing expertise literally makes certain thought patterns more efficient than others. You want to know what stuck in a rut looks like? Look at the brain of an expert."

But with chess, a funny thing happens: once you punch through this pocket of journeymen who fall into the quicksand of the familiar, you reach a rating at which players again see the optimal solutions even when presented with more obvious alternatives. In short, at the level of chess masters, you again encounter flexibility. These master chess players somehow have their cake and eat it too: they aren't in the constant crisis of novice uncertainty, but neither are they bound by their experience to the obvious plays. Similarly, in any field, it's this flexible, as opposed to rigid, expertise that allows masters to push the cutting edge.

So let's look at expertise in two parts—first at how to develop expertise and then at how to ensure it doesn't shackle you to rigidity.

In a series of experiments that have come to define the modern understanding of expertise, Feltovich, along with colleagues Michelene Chi, Robert Glaser, and Ernest Rees, explored the development of expertise in another brainy field—physics—asking the question: How do novice physicists differ from experts? And more generally: What makes one person an expert and another a novice?

Here's how they're similar: when Feltovich asked experts (physics professors) and novices (freshmen) to categorize twenty-four physics problems pulled from a college textbook on Newtonian mechanics, both experts and novices generated about 8.5 categories, and both took about thirty-seven seconds per problem to do it. But novices tended to group problems into, for example, ones with springs, or ones with inclined planes, or by words in the problem like friction or center of mass—the "surface features" or "form" of the problem. On the other hand, experts categorized problems by Newton's Second Law, or Conservation of Mass and Energy, or Conservation of Angular Momentum—in other words, by function. Novices notice form, whereas experts notice function.

And even without a principle in mind, physics novices tended to immediately reach for plug-and-play equations that seemed likely to offer quick solutions. If a first equation didn't work out, novices scrolled to the next as if falling down through a decision tree of equations, bouncing from one branch to the next until getting hung up on the branch that eventually solved the problem . . . or hitting the ground.

On the other hand, after reading a problem and before reaching for equations, experts inserted a step: they visualized the problem according to its functional components. For example, what were the important interrelationships between an inclined plane, a block sliding down it, friction, and gravity?

Chess experts have similar expert vision. After glancing at a board, not only can chess experts reproduce positions more accurately than novices, but—like physics experts—they can describe the important functional interrelationships between pieces. Experts literally see a system's function.

But the same ability to boil a problem down to its functional parts is one source of expert rigidity. Specifically, representing a problem as the skeleton of its functional features is great, as long as you don't disregard any functional features. And sometimes, that's what experts do: they know what should matter, what usually matters, and their stripped-down visualization excludes small, strange things that happen to matter in just this particular case. Sometimes experts fail to detect unusualness and may even shove aside things that don't fit their streamlined view.

Feltovich calls this blinkering "reductive bias," and there are factors that make experts especially prone to it. For example, if a situation is changing, an expert's reductive snapshot might define the situation at one moment but fail to describe a new, changed version. Or experts may simplify things into categories they don't entirely fit, like the 2011 Pittsburgh Steelers who considered Denver's Tim Tebow a rushing quarterback instead of somewhere on the rushing side of a spectrum between throwing and rushing quarterbacks, thus leaving themselves open to a couple of decisive deep throws. Or experts may oversimplify the possibilities—for example, a doctor overlooking rare diseases in favor of the ones he diagnoses every day.

In other words, some experts—like journeymen chess players, doctors faced with a rare disease, physics students, and NFL defensive coordinators—are good at dealing efficiently with the situations they know. But their reductionist world views lead to failure when the worlds they know throw curveballs. Who knew Tim Tebow could hit the broad side of a barn?

How can experts avoid falling into this trap? According to Feltovich, the key to avoiding rigid expertise is constantly seeking new experiences. "This means deliberate practice," he says. "You're constantly aware of your capability, constantly looking for weaknesses, and fundamentally always trying to identify them and make them better."

Which brings us to our second step toward flexible expertise: to develop flexible expertise, focus on your weaknesses and not your strengths.

Alexandra Michel, professor of management at the USC Marshall School of Business and author of the book *Bullish on Uncertainty,* says this constant newness is the strategy of especially innovative businesses. "Google and Goldman Sachs hire English majors and concert pianists and then ask for a cash-flow analysis by the next morning. An expert knows it can't be done, but a pianist marshals organizational resources in new and creative ways to accomplish the task," she says. These companies, she says, constantly push employees into new situations in which they're uncertain, specifically to avoid the development of rigid, domain-specific expertise. For example, she describes how Goldman might move a developing mergers expert from the New York to the Frankfurt office where the rules are just different enough to keep Ms. Mergers on her toes.

"Unusualness is becoming the norm," says Feltovich. The employees at Goldman and Google are poised to surf the tide of the world's increasing unusualness, for a concert pianist turned business analyst really isn't a novice—they've mastered the process of expertise, if not the domain-specific experience. And unmooring expertise from its domain—by deliberate practice of new experiences that force us from our comfort zones—allows for the flexibility of a novice with the approach of an expert. Flexible, domain-general expertise develops as long as you're forced to continue bringing your intelligence and not just your experience to bear on new problems.

"If you're never satisfied, if you're great you can become greater," says Feltovich. "That's what divides the good from the truly great."

DELIBERATE PRACTICE

Florida State researcher K. Anders Ericsson shows that it's not only experience that creates expertise but a step-by-step method of sculpting experience that he calls *deliberate practice*. To Ericsson, famous for his theory that 10,000 hours of practice creates expertise in any field, the four-step path to expertise includes performing your skill, monitoring your performance, evaluating your success, and figuring out how to do it better next time. Completing only the first step—performing the skill itself—leads to automated, low-level, rote performance in which you perform the skill the same way every time. Monitoring, evaluating, and adjusting your skill allows you to modify it after every pass, helping skill evolve toward expertise. So you'll need to find your weaknesses.

Tennis players and musicians hire coaches and teachers to ferret out their weaknesses so they can work on them between performances. You should do the same, only you might need to be your own coach. Here's how:

1. List an activity.

2. In the format of a family tree, below the activity list its major skills. For example, if the activity were tennis, you might list serve, forehand, backhand, volley, and footwork.

3. Now continue working down the family tree, listing the increasingly minute subskills that make up each major skill. For example, you might list below "serve" the components planning, toss, body tension, footwork, swing, placement, spin, and follow-through.

4. Once you've broken the activity into its divisible microcomponents, circle the ones on which you struggle. You've now isolated your weaknesses and it's time for deliberate practice to make them better.

DELIBERATE PERFORMANCE

Let's face it: unless you're a professional musician or athlete, you might not have time for deliberate practice. Luckily, psychologists Gary Klein and Peter Fadde suggest another way of developing expertise, a process they call deliberate *performance*. According to their model, we can develop expertise during the work or play we already do. Their training has four parts—estimation, experimentation, extrapolation, and explanation. Every day this week, choose to focus on one of these four E's, described below.

Estimation: From estimating time needed for troop movements to predicting businesses' annual revenues to guessing at penalty kick direction or prophesying how much time items on a meeting agenda will take, estimating outcomes allows you to check your expertise. Fadde and Klein show that working to understand what creates the difference between your estimates and actual outcomes allows you to train it. List an estimation you made today. Now list how far off it was. Why the difference?

Experimentation: There are three subcategories here—exploring without a goal, performing a purposeful action, and testing a hypothesis. No matter the type of experimentation you engage in, "Learning through experimentation is good for both maintaining and developing expertise," write Fadde and Klein. They show that even if experimentation results in a (reasonably small) step back in performance, it can help make flexible expertise and so is an investment in improved future performance. What kind of experimentation did you do today?

Extrapolation: Air traffic controllers and mountain climbers keep databases of accidents and near misses, allowing them to learn from others' mistakes in fields where it's too costly to make their own. Likewise, "Learners can ask themselves where they, or somebody they are observing, could have lost a client or a patient or a negotiation and learn deeply from those real or imagined near misses," write Fadde and Klein. What did you learn from experience today, yours or others?

Explanation: Get feedback. Do a good postmortem. Listen to the opinions of colleagues, clients, experts, or your inner compass to list at least three things that went right and one thing that went wrong with one of your actions or decisions today.

EXERCISE 26

EXPERT MEMORY

Experts have not only "know-what and know-how, but know-why," write psychologists Daniel Kimball and Keith Holyoak. In fact, an expert's know-why can sometimes even elbow aside bits of know-what. For example, classic studies of computer programmers show that expert coders have great memories for the chunks of script that create a program's function, but have worse recall than mid-level performers of the specific lines of code they used to get there. Likewise, baseball experts use more of what Kimball and Holyoak call "goal-related propositions" when recalling an inning of play. For example, an expert might talk about laying down a bunt to advance a runner from first to second so the runner could score on an outfield single, whereas the nonexpert might just recall the facts of a bunt and the runner's advance, but not the reasons for it. And medical experts forget a patient's specifics in favor of the functional components that lead to a diagnosis. All of this forgetting of specifics in favor of functions is what Kimball and Holyoak call an "increase in selectivity and abstraction."

How do experts get this particular brand of memory? Well, most researchers think that experts compare novel situations with "schema" stored in long-term memory. You load patterns into your personal Rolodex and then constantly compare new experiences to these stored ones. When there's a near enough match between present and pattern, experts recognize the schema and know how to act.

Chess is an easy and much-studied example and so it's a nice forum in which to practice developing this expert memory. That said, you could just as easily design your own expertise-training schema for common work dilemmas, parenting challenges, social conundrums, or the like—any domain that can be categorized into common types that can be recognized with practice.

First copy and cut out the following ten boards (or make ten "schema" for the non-chess domain of your choice). What are its functional components—in this case, what piece positions allow white to checkmate in one move? In play or in life, you'll have to recognize these functional components even when obscured by what researchers call *surface features*—namely other, unimportant, pieces on the board. Now as you flip through your new deck, name the checkmates—for example, the first might be "Two-pawn attack." Once you can name all these checkmates and their functional components, search online for images of random chessboard positions. Which of your ten checkmates seems the best, closest option? Then, in your life, try to start noticing the similarity in situations you encounter to the schemas you've stored. This quick recognition of schema is a major component of expert performance.

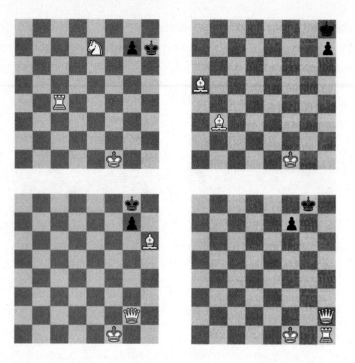

REDUCTIVE BIAS IN MEDICAL DIAGNOSIS

In winter, the town of Kotzebue, Alaska, is accessible only by air or snow machine and is home to about three thousand people, mostly Inupiat Eskimos. As you can imagine, in these lovely Alaskan winters, people tend to crowd together indoors hoping to avoid unpleasant things like hypothermia and death. And so when one person gets the sniffles, it spreads like wildfire through the population. The same is true of tuberculosis, which was the state's leading cause of death until 1950. On National Public Radio, Dr. Michael Cooper described patients he saw in Kotzebue as recently as 2009 presenting with a persistent cough, night sweats, and weight loss, and lamented that "TB was rarely on my list of diagnoses when I would see a patient. I hate to admit that. And as I look back now, I go through these patients some nights and I think, that patient could have had TB, and why didn't I at least do this? Wasn't I even aware of it?"

Now working for Alaska's Department of Health, it's Cooper's job to lower the state's unusually high rate of tuberculosis. How does he do it? By combating the blindness he experienced as an expert. Like a counter-intuitive chess move, tuberculosis wasn't on his list of diagnoses and so despite indicative symptoms, he and other Alaskan doctors tended to overlook the possibility of the disease.

10,000 HOURS OF PRACTICE

You've probably heard K. Anders Ericsson's theory that 10,000 hours of practice in any discipline creates expertise. In 2010 this inspirational message—you can do anything you put your mind to!—convinced Portland, Oregon, photographer Dan McLaughlin to quit his job and devote forty hours a week toward the 10,000 hours of practice he hopes will make him a professional golfer. McLaughlin started from scratch—not as in "was a 'scratch' golfer," but rather in 2010 he didn't even know if he was a left- or right-handed golfer. The only club he owned was a putter. Still, his everyman's quest for glory landed him a sponsorship from Nike, a PGA-certified golf coach, and an Olympic strength trainer. On June 9, 2012, Dan's daily check-in at his blog read, "Warmed up and practiced some at Heron Lakes then played the Great Blue course again. Was a slow start today, but had a solid streak on the back nine after doubling a par 3. 7,065 [hours] remain. Random Stat: shot an 80 from the blue tees." At his current pace, Dan will finish his 10,000 hours sometime in 2016. For Dan's sake, it will be nice if Ericsson's 10,000 hours theory holds up.

CHAPTER 8

WORKING MEMORY

Sorry, this one chapter may not be beyond IQ at all. That's because the ability to hold and manipulate information in the front of your mind is such a central component of intelligence that any gains you make may accidentally overflow into your testable IQ. Oh well, you can't bake a cake without breaking eggs. But IQ isn't the only area into which working memory overflows—it's a major engine of problem solving, logic, multitasking, performance under pressure, and other skills that require analytical thinking. In short, your working memory is where you *work*, and building a larger workshop is a pathway to a better brain.

You've probably heard about the seven "chunks" of your working memory, but current thought is that our working memories may be fixed at four rather than seven chunks. With training, however, you can expand each of those chunks to hold more info. In fact, bigger working-memory chunk size is a major component of the expertise we saw in the previous chapter. Chess experts can glance at a board and reproduce the piece positions because each chunk of a chess expert's working memory can hold three to six pieces, whereas the working memory of a novice can hold only one piece per chunk. From electrical engineers to baseball aficionados, each chunk of an expert's working memory stores more information than a novice's.

You too can develop an expert's working memory, and researchers at the University of Michigan, including John Jonides, Martin Buschkuehl, and Susanne Jaeggi, know how. To boost working memory, they use a task called the n-back. There are a couple of variations, but essentially the n-back asks subjects to monitor a series of stuff—like a string of letters—and report the letter that was 2-back or 3-back or 4-back in the string. It's so simple! Only, it's not at all simple.

"It's difficult to come up with strategies for the n-back," says Buschkuehl. "For example, when we asked participants to tell us how they did it, we saw they really didn't know—they had a hard time naming their strategy. And the other thing was, there was no common way they did it. There wasn't a single strategy we could identify." This strategyless-ness is a prerequisite of any task that truly trains the brain—it means that instead of storing the rote behavior in your implicit memory, you continue to struggle with it in your working memory.

"Furthermore, we adjusted the difficulty of the task depending on your performance, switching from a two-back to three-back. That changes the task a little bit, makes it even harder to stick to the same strategy," Buschkuehl says.

The Michigan group trained subjects on the n-back twenty-five minutes a day for nineteen days, and lo and behold when the training period was over, subjects showed improved working memory and also higher testable IQs. When the researchers imaged subjects' brains with fMRI, what they found was a little counterintuitive—the brains of people trained on the n-back looked less rather than more active in relevant areas during working-memory tasks. There was less blood flow and the brain used less energy. Rather than the expected beefing-up, this very physical brain training looks like beefing-down—an increase in efficiency rather than raw power.

Gaining this efficiency isn't easy. But it's specifically this struggle of lifting a mental dumbbell until you can't lift it anymore that will eventually allow you to pack more information into the four chunks of your working memory.

EXERCISE 27
DIGIT SPAN

Before you train your working memory, test it using the venerable digit-span task, which is a component of many psychological assessments. Then once you've done some training, come back and take the digit-span test again. Did you improve? The average score for people aged twenty-one to thirty is just over 5 digits; for people aged fifty and over it's about 4.5 digits.

Here's the simple test:

Either make five copies of the numbers on page 108 and then cut them to make a deck of 45 number cards or write your own block numbers on scrap paper. In either case, you want a deck of about 40 to 50 random digits. Shuffle the deck. Now start with strings of three numbers—from the top of your shuffled deck, flip three cards, one at a time, looking for about a second at each before laying it face-down. Remember and repeat out loud the order of these numbers and if you're unsure, check your answer (or, ideally, have a partner check you). Continue flipping, memorizing, and repeating three-card strings until you've finished the deck. This should be relatively easy. But now try it with four-digit "chunks." Still easy? Try five-digit strings and then six. Can you do seven? Eight? At some point you'll start to break down.

When you fail to correctly recall more than 50 percent of the strings during one full pass through the deck (or a couple of passes if your digit span is inhumanly long), you've reached failure. The previous string length is your digit span. Write down your score!

Now try it in reverse. If the first three cards you flip over are 3, 6, and 2, you should report, "2, 6, 3." Most people can store about one fewer digit in the reverse-digit test than they can in the forward condition. Write down this score as well.

1	2	3
4	5	6
7	8	9

EXERCISE 28
N-BACK

Some exercises in this book teach you to recognize the processes beneath your thoughts and then once you can see these patterns, you're immediately "trained." The n-back isn't one of them. Instead, the n-back trains working memory like dumbbell curls train biceps. It takes time and consistent practice. As seen earlier in the chapter, researchers

Jonides, Jaeggi, and Buschkuehl found measurable results with a program of about twenty minutes a day for about twenty days. They also showed that this training *scales,* meaning that more training equals more gain. So with this exercise and the next, you'll need to commit to a focused schedule and give it a few weeks of practice before you can expect results. But if you *do* put in the hard work needed, you really will affect the basic capabilities of your brain.

Here's how:

- Create your n-back viewer: place the right edge of a note card along the bold line in the first strip on page 110. Now cut two windows in the note card so that you can see the bold-bordered boxes containing the star and the square.

- Note the two triangles and a circle covered by the note card. Now slide your homemade n-back viewer along the strip of symbols one column at a time, memorizing the symbols as you go. Here's the insidious part: every time you slide the card one symbol to the right, report the symbol that was in the previous box in the top row, and two boxes back in the bottom row.

- After you report the 1-back (top row) and 2-back (bottom row) symbols, slide your note card over the next column and your cutout boxes will allow you to check your answers.

- Stay in the optimal training zone. If 1-back and 2-back are too easy, increase the difficulty by cutting out windows farther away from your note card's edge to report symbols that are 3-back or 4-back. Also consider cutting out the n-back strips and laying them together to make new, longer patterns.

- As spectacularly entertaining as this surely is, keep at it for twenty minutes.

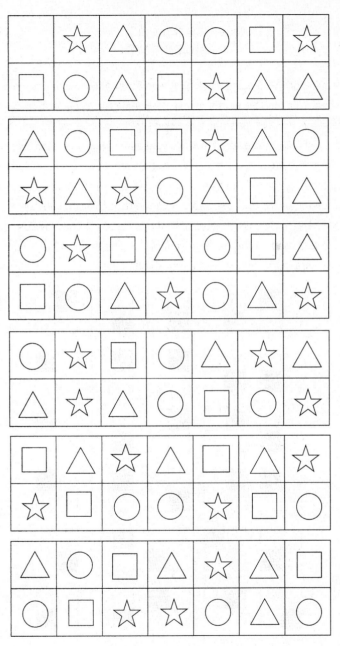

EXERCISE 29
SIMON SAYS

Remember the beeping, flashing Simon Says lightboxes of your youth? Here's a paper version that packs the same cerebral punch, this time with the purpose of training working memory. Use your hand or a piece of paper to cover all the following boxes. Now reveal the first box and then quickly cover it. Use your other hand to push an imaginary button in an upper-right quadrant on your desk or on your lap. Now scroll the paper to reveal two grids (and then cover them!). Use your free hand to repeat the pattern. Continue revealing one new box each turn and tapping the pattern from the beginning until failure. Start anywhere in the sequence of boxes and try again.

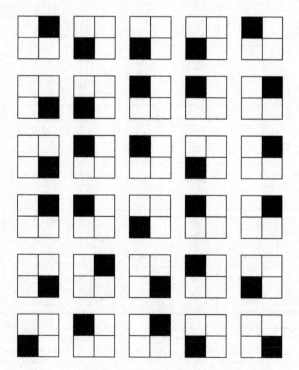

CHAPTER 9

KEEPING INTELLIGENCE

People who have gone to college stay sharp longer than people who haven't. Likewise, a job that requires navigating complex relationships, setting up elaborate systems, or dealing with difficult people and problems can push back brain decay by a decade. The reason for this is the very simple secret of cognitive involvement: the more you use your brain, the longer you'll be able to use it.

What if you didn't go to college or spent your college years trying to kill brain cells rather than grow them? Luckily, the choices you make in your twenties aren't the only way to protect your brain into your sixties, seventies, and beyond. It turns out that going back to school in midlife has the same brain-protective effect as attending college at the traditional age. Even better: researchers Margie Lachman and Patricia Tun of Brandeis University found that you can self-train your brain just as effectively as you would through college or a demanding job. In their studies of senior citizens who hadn't gone to college, they saw one common factor among the most overachieving brains: the people with "cognitively protected" brains were those who challenged themselves through a lifestyle that included reading, writing, attending lectures, and doing word puzzles—in other words, they followed a self-imposed regimen of cognitive involvement.

If you're sold already, flip to the end of this chapter for exercises to keep you cognitively involved—although, in fact, most of the exercises in this book should make your neurons crackle in a protective way. But cognitive involvement is only one tine of a three-pronged approach to brain health in later life. The second tine is a healthy body. "What is good for our hearts is also good for our heads," says Archana Singh-Manoux, lead author of the Whitehall II study, which followed the aging of 10,308 British Civil Service workers. Whitehall II showed that obesity and hypertension in middle age leads to cognitive decline later in life. In fact, your cardiovascular health in middle age is even more important for your later brain health than the same risk factors in old age itself. Likewise, cardiovascular exercise, moderate alcohol consumption, and even living in a good neighborhood can affect your body and so your mind.

Finally, in addition to cognitive involvement and a healthy body, the third tine of cognitive protection is personality. The massive study known as MIDUS (Midlife in the United States) shows that remaining calm in the face of stress, feeling more in control of your life, optimism, and openness to new experiences are markers of cognitively above-average seniors. But the most powerful part of personality is social interaction. Nothing forces the brain to work like interacting with other brains. And all these personality factors are interconnected—more social interaction leads to more brainpower, which leads in turn to more interaction, and so a rising tide floats all boats. The other fair analogy is to a house of cards: allow one aspect of your personality to slip and all domains of brain health can come tumbling down along with it.

So safeguarding your cognitive resources requires a long-term lifestyle commitment, not just to using your brain but to using your body and staying social as well. The last two are up to you. Meanwhile, let's get your cognitive involvement jump-started with the following exercises.

ACTIVE

A study known as ACTIVE, which stands for Advanced Cognitive Training for Independent and Vital Elderly, shows the effects of brain training in later life. The study split 2,832 people into three groups and offered ten one-hour training sessions in either memory, processing speed, or reasoning. Five years later, some exciting results were published in the *Journal of the American Medical Association*: while training in memory and processing speed didn't seem to have much effect, *reasoning* training not only improved the participants' cognitive skills but helped them continue to live independently. This is a big deal: this cognitive training improved not only subjects' brains but their lives.

There were two major pieces of the ACTIVE reasoning training: learning to reason about everyday information and training pattern recognition skills. You can approximate the training in everyday reasoning simply by making sure you understand the information you happen to run across in your everyday life—for example, nutrition panels on cereal boxes, recipe directions, dosage instructions on over-the-counter medicines, medical insurance information, taxi rates, and so on. When you're hit with information, you have a choice: you can struggle to understand it, or you can let it slide past while groking just enough to get by. ACTIVE shows that working to fully understand the information that comes your way helps you keep the ability to understand it.

The second major section of the ACTIVE reasoning training was learning to work with patterns—the old recognize-and-predict-the-next thing. It seems like a trivial skill, but according to Thelma and Louis Thurstone, who pioneered pattern-recognition research in the 1940s (and apparently provided the names for a popular movie), seeing patterns tests our ability to "solve problems, foresee consequences, analyze a situation on the basis of past experience, and make and carry out plans according to recognized facts." The skill is anything but trivial.

The ACTIVE trial tested participants' pattern recognition, trained them, and then tested them again to check for improvement. We'll do the same. Start by testing your pattern-recognition skills by writing the next letter in each pattern of the pretest below. Then flip to the back of this book for answers and training before returning here to take the test. Afterward, more training is only an Internet search away—just Google the phrase "pattern-recognition test" and you'll find plenty of options including picture and number patterns. For brain health in late life, the more pattern practice the merrier.

PATTERN-RECOGNITION PRETEST

1. bcbcbcbcb . . .
2. fffggghhhiiijj . . .
3. gfefededcdcb . . .
4. tubcuvcdvwd . . .
5. cexdfxegxfhx . . .
6. hipijqjkrklslm . . .
7. efbghbijbklb . . .
8. hijkijkljklmklm . . .
9. tpqtqrtrststttutu . . .
10. pmopnopooppo . . .
11. xbqxcrxdsxe . . .

12. abvabuabtabsab . . .

13. tontattonta . . .

14. emoeroenoeqoeoo . . .

15. eftufguvghvwh . . .

PATTERN RECOGNITION TEST

1. bikbabbikba . . .

2. jihihghgfgfe . . .

3. rsastbtucuvdvw . . .

4. iufiuwiugiuviuhiu . . .

5. pqcrsctucvwc . . .

6. thththththh . . .

7. histijtujkuv . . .

8. pqrsqrstrstustuvtu . . .

9. nopnpqnqrnrsns . . .

10. bcdccddcdecd . . .

11. gikhjkikkjlkk . . .

12. lllmmmnnnooopp . . .

13. semsfnsgoshps . . .

14. lmcdmndenoefopf . . .

15. cdtcdscdrcdqcdpcd . . .

| | | | | | | | | | | | | | EXERCISE 31 | | | | | | | | | | | | | | | | | | | |

A COGNITIVELY INVOLVED LIFESTYLE

Does a crossword a day keep brain decay away? Well, yes and no. A crossword forces you to mine your memory for a wide range of information, and by recalling things like another name for a sewing case (etui), tool handle (haft), or Spartan serf (helot), you reinforce both specific memories and the process of remembering itself. This helps you hold your baseline *crystalized intelligence*—that is, your store of knowledge. In that way, crosswords are a whole lot better than Sudoku, which, once you've learned the techniques, is effectively a rote exercise in filling boxes with numbers.

But if you want to slow the decline of *fluid intelligence*—your ability to *reason* with these pieces of crystalized intelligence—you'll have to go further than the crossword. In fact, once you understand a puzzle's directions and how you should go about solving it, you've harvested the majority of its ability to boost or maintain fluid intelligence. At that point, actually solving the puzzle becomes practice without much purpose. So instead of playing your favorite smartphone game into the ground, try to download a new one every week. And instead of getting stuck in the rut of one type of favorite brain-training puzzle, look for a new kind every session. Skipping around this book is a good start. And once you've exhausted the puzzle types here, continue to search out not only new repetitions of puzzle types you know but new types entirely. Make it a practice to periodically hop online in search of games or puzzles with novel directions. Maybe make it a once-a-week ritual. And then once you've got the instructions nailed, pivot away in search of a fresh mental challenge.

EXERCISE 32
A COGNITIVELY KIND LIFESTYLE

In addition to puzzles and challenges that directly kick-start your neurons, certain lifestyle choices lead to healthy aging in the brain. Consider incorporating the following brain-protective tips into your daily routine:

- **Exercise:** In his presidential address to the 2010 meeting of the American Heart Association, Dr. Ralph Sacco said that nearly any measure of brain health is related to heart health. From multitasking to attention to psychomotor speed to brain volume to measures of general intelligence, people who have good vascular risk scores and better cardiac indexes have better brain scores, too. The reason for this is simple: your brain likes oxygen and nutrients. Your heart and vascular system *give* it oxygen and nutrients. And so what's good for your heart is good for your brain. Light exercise is best. For example, a study of older adults found that thirty to fifty minutes of brisk walking four times a week increased blood flow to the brain by 15 percent compared to sedentary subjects.

- **Diet:** Oregon State University researchers asked which goodies in the blood predict a sharp brain. Even controlling for age, education, and all the socioeconomic factors you can imagine, older adults whose blood contained fish-oil fatty acids and vitamins B, C, D, and E had 17 percent better scores on cognitive tests and 37 percent larger brains than subjects whose blood was a coagulated mess of trans-fats. Other likely brain foods include antioxidants (found in berries), choline (found in eggs), uridine monophosphate (found in beets), and docosahexaenoic acid (another component of fish oil). Experts aren't sure whether this brain-boosting diet acts directly on the brain or if benefits come by way of the heart—in other words, these foods may simply be good for heart health, which in turn is good for brain health. Either way, there's mounting evidence that what you eat affects how you think.

- **Drink:** You've heard this before, but it bears repeating: moderate alcohol consumption, and especially drinking red wine, has been definitively shown by the Mayo Clinic and elsewhere to be good for your heart—and again, what's good for your heart is good for your brain.

- **Sleep:** A 5,431-person study found that six, seven, or eight hours of sleep are all fine for the brain—as long as sleep habits never change! People who changed their sleep habits in middle age, either getting more or fewer hours per night, hurt their brains in the form of lower inductive reasoning, vocabulary, phonemic and semantic fluency, and overall cognitive ability. As long as you're not getting more than nine hours or fewer than six hours of sleep per night, stick with your current schedule. Oh, and your brain likes a good nap.

THE AGING BALANCE OF FLUID AND CRYSTALIZED INTELLIGENCE

From your mid-twenties until about age sixty you sit on a plateau of maximum brainpower. But this plateau is anything but static. Creative ability, including the research that leads to Nobel Prizes in mathematics and physics, as well as achievement in lyric poetry, the arts, and music peak in the late twenties or early thirties. You can see this in the Dallas Lifespan Brain Study, which is currently following 550 people as they age from twenty to ninety. Results from eleven of fourteen cognitive tests look like a playground slide—three tests of processing speed, four tests of working memory, and four tests of long-term memory start high in twenty-year-olds and then uniformly fade as you age.

But as your fluid intelligence declines, you replace it with crystalized intelligence—knowledge and experience—and until your sixties, gains in crystalized intelligence balance losses in fluid intelligence. So while the ingredients of your cognitive success change, your overall intelligence stays generally even. You can see the results of this second, knowledge-based success in the mean ages of Fortune 500 CEOs, which are clustered between fifty and fifty-nine, and in the median age of US presidents when they took office—fifty-four years, eleven months.

NEUROBIOLOGY OF THE AGING BRAIN

Why does your fluid intelligence start to decrease as you enter middle age? First, your frontal lobes shrink—they're associated with decision-making. Second, the white matter that insulates neurons, keeping their signals crisp, becomes more porous. Third, the brain accumulates gunk in the form of a protein called beta-amyloid—the substance that runs amok in the brains of people with Alzheimer's. And finally, the corpus callosum that forms the barrier between the right and left hemispheres of the brain starts to break down. In extreme cases, as in multiple sclerosis, the corpus callosum decays entirely, leading to "mirror movements" in which instead of one hand moving, both move. Before their corpus collosum has fully formed, babies do this, too.

A SURPRISING CAUSE OF SENIOR MOMENTS

fMRI shows that when asked to report details of faces, older subjects can't help but process background details as well as the faces. And when interrupted, older brains have difficulty reestablishing connection with what they were doing. All said, older people are more likely to take in irrelevant information and be sidetracked by irrelevant tasks. Thus, "senior moments" are a problem not of memory but of attention. *To help combat this loss of attention, flip to this book's exercises that train executive function.*

CHAPTER 10

WISDOM

Jiddu Krishnamurti, Indian American spiritual guru of the 1940s through the 1980s, was quite the jokester. According to Krishnamurti's still-functional website, one of the funnies he liked to tell was the story of a young man who leaves home to look for wisdom. The man goes to a well-known guru who lives on the banks of a river. "Please, sir," he says to the old man, "allow me to stay with you. I want to learn the truth from you." The guru agrees and so the young man spends five years washing the guru's clothes, cooking for him, and performing all kinds of tasks for the presumably wise old teacher. And after five years, he says to the master, "I've spent five years with you but I still don't know the truth and haven't learned a thing. So if you don't mind, I'll leave you. Perhaps I can find another teacher from whom I can learn more about the truth."

"Sure," says the old man, "go right ahead."

So the young man goes off and finds several other gurus, from whom he learns various tricks. After another five years have passed, the man remembers his old teacher and goes to visit him.

"So what have you learned?" the old man asks. And his former student tells him that he can walk on hot coals, levitate, and pointing at the river, says proudly, "And I can walk on the waters of that river to the opposite shore!"

"It took you five years to learn that?" exclaims the old master. "Didn't you know that not more than fifty yards from here, you can take the ferry boat across for two pence?"

Please take as much time as you need to control your paroxysms of hilarity. Are you finished? OK. While the joke isn't necessarily LOL funny, it makes an important point: intelligence and wisdom are not the same thing. In this story, the young man returns to his old master with learning and skills—the trappings of intelligence—but without wisdom. But if wisdom isn't intelligence, then what is it?

First, it's a paradox: wisdom is one of the most studied and admired human abilities in ancient traditions ranging from the Greek philosophers to the Hindu Vedas. But of the skills in this book, it's probably the least represented in modern labs. The few modern experts working on wisdom disagree on exactly what it is, but can generally get behind the idea of wisdom as the sum of cognitive, reflective, and emotional components.

In the cognitive component, a wise person comprehends the truth—the world as it is, unclouded by the way we want it to be. In the reflective component, the wise person thinks objectively and from perspectives outside that of self-centeredness. Finally, the emotional component of wisdom trades depression, anger, and hatred for empathy, sympathy, and compassion. Science considers the reflective component the keystone for developing the other two—if you can reflect from outside your own point of view, you can learn to see the truth and feel/act accordingly.

For example, in the lead-up to the 2008 presidential election, psychologists Ethan Kross and Igor Grossmann asked strongly liberal and strongly conservative subjects to think about what the world would be like if their preferred candidate lost. Some were asked to reason as US citizens and some were asked to reason as if they lived in Iceland. Reasoning with distance—from outside the self-centered viewpoint—allowed the erstwhile Icelanders to recognize that no matter who won the election, the world was unlikely to fly from its orbit and spiral into the sun. People who went to Iceland in their minds were also more likely than immersed observers to list their contact info on a sheet gathering names for a bipartisan discussion group. In short, metaphorical distance allowed the "Icelanders" to act more wisely than the group that reasoned from an embedded perspective.

So now we see not only what wisdom is but the first step to achieving it: reasoning from many perspectives, and specifically from outside your own. Wisdom is not all about you.

Perhaps, as popular opinion holds, the second ingredient of wisdom is age? Science has asked this question, and it turns out there's a somewhat nuanced answer. See, in nearly any measurable decision-making task researchers throw at them, younger people act more wisely than older ones. With youth comes wisdom; with age comes foolishness.

But there's one kind of decision-making game the elderly totally dominate.

"In many real-world contexts, our present choices often determine our future possibilities," writes Darrell Worthy and his colleagues in a 2011 article for the journal *Psychological Science*. In his game, subjects had to extract an ever-decreasing amount of virtual oxygen from Mars. One extraction method pulled more oxygen per round but quickly degraded the ability to extract more—it was like eating chocolate cake: good right away but with decreasing gains in the long run. Another method was slow and steady, extracting less oxygen per round but only slowly degrading subjects' ability to harvest oxygen in later rounds—it was like eating a quinoa-chard salad: joyless in the moment but with benefits over time. Older subjects chose the "salad" option and thus won the game by maximizing the long-term payoff of the system as a whole.

It turns out young people are better at associating choices with their direct values, but older people are better at describing how "various options and their associated rewards are connected to one another," Worthy writes.

With age comes wisdom—at least in the system-wide, slow-burn sense of the term.

But as the venerable Robert Sternberg points out, with age, "Some people become truly wise and some become old fools." If that's the case, there must then be even another ingredient. What makes this difference? Maybe as Aeschylus wrote, "Wisdom comes alone through suffering"? Maybe it's the accumulation of suffering that brings wisdom, and those who become old fools instead of growing wise simply haven't suffered enough?

There's a bit of truthiness in this. In 2001, a study at the University of Michigan showed that women who went through major upheavals in love or career in their thirties generally had more wisdom in their fifties than those who coasted through middle age on waters of serenity. That is, as long as one important thing was true: overall, good experiences had to outweigh bad experiences. Suffering leads to wisdom only as long as it's balanced by joy. Otherwise, you can live as wretchedly as you like without gaining wisdom to show for it.

So we've talked about a few important factors in building wisdom: perspective, age, and joy overbalancing suffering. Mix them all together and you get what Sternberg calls the genesis of wisdom: "The main way wisdom is created is the extent to which you learn through your experience." It's not just the fact of accumulated experience that creates wisdom, but what we get from these experiences. "It's how much you observe, how much you want to learn, how much you process," says Sternberg.

Krishnamurti summarizes this recipe for wisdom in slightly different words: "Meditation is to be aware of every thought and of every feeling, never to say it is right or wrong but just to watch it and move with it. In that watching you begin to understand the whole movement of thought and feeling. And out of this awareness comes silence."

Reflect on the experience of these words, Grasshopper, and wisdom you will find.

THE WISDOM OF PROVERBS

Paul Baltes of the Max Planck Institute, one of the founders of the modern study of wisdom, showed that wisdom really can be captured by proverbs. Unfortunately, he showed that the opposite is true too—proverbs may also crystalize rules of thumb that make us feel better, without necessarily recommending wise thoughts, feelings, or actions.

The wise among us know the difference.

In fact, Baltes showed both that wise people consistently choose wise proverbs over attractive alternatives (whereas *unwise* people are suckered by the panaceas), and that by reflecting on the difference between the two we can develop this wisdom. Here's a test similar to one pioneered by Baltes in 1999:

In each of the following situations, choose the proverb that best represents the wise action or attitude. Some will seem ambiguous at first and, of course, the choice is supposed to be difficult. The true training in this exercise comes from the explanation in the answers section at the back of the book—but to avoid spoilers, please answer these before you flip to the back for the punch line.

1. If something matters to me . . .

   A) Procrastination is the thief of time.

   B) Time will tell.

2. When a worthwhile task proves difficult . . .

   A) Don't change horses midstream.

   B) Enough is enough.

3. When an entrenched practice proves not to be a *best* practice . . .

   A) Don't shut the stable door after the horse has bolted.

   B) A stitch in time saves nine.

4. When struggling to decide . . .

   A) Between two stools you fall to the ground.

   B) Tomorrow is another day.

5. When feeling spread thin . . .

   A) Enough is as good as a feast.

   B) Jack of all trades, master of none.

6. When things fail to click into place . . .

   A) It's no use crying over spilt milk.

   B) When there's no wind, grab the oars.

7. When your goal may require a contentious struggle . . .

   A) Leave well enough alone.

   B) Strike when the iron is hot.

8. When presented with a setback . . .

   A) If at first you don't succeed, try, try again.

   B) Time heals all wounds.

9. When a first attempt fails . . .

   A) Desperate times call for desperate measures.

   B) After a rain comes sunshine.

10. When you have set something in motion that is failing . . .

    A) Easy come, easy go.

    B) God helps those who help themselves.

11. In the face of many goals and limited resources . . .

   A) Variety is the spice of life.

   B) Those who follow every path never reach any destination.

12. When things seem more difficult than you imagined they would be . . .

   A) Practice makes perfect.

   B) Good things come to those who wait.

13. When looking ahead at impending challenges . . .

   A) Don't cross a bridge till you come to it.

   B) Make hay while the sun is shining.

14. When forced to choose between two alternatives . . .

   A) You can't have your cake and eat it, too.

   B) Good things come to those who wait.

15. When setbacks force you to revise your goal . . .

   A) Those without a horse walk.

   B) Out of sight, out of mind.

16. When time is tight . . .

   A) Everyone has his cross to bear.

   B) One can't have everything.

17. When one method fails . . .

   A) Man gets used to everything.

   B) There are many hands; what one cannot do, the other will.

18. When presented with unforeseen challenges that make a goal seem more difficult than you imagined . . .

   A) Don't lose the ship for a hap'orth of tar.

   B) Everything comes to him who waits.

IMAGINE WISDOM

Paul Baltes writes, "There exist cognitive strategies, readily adopt-able by most individuals, that can increase the expression of wisdom-related knowledge." One of these strategies is imagination. In a 1996 study, Baltes showed that people presented with a life problem who then imagine a conversation with a significant other act with more wisdom than those who spend a similar amount of time learning academically about the idea of wisdom. In a follow-up, Baltes and his colleagues asked people to imagine floating to different countries on a cloud and to reflect on the cultures and peoples they visit. Afterward, these dreamers gave measurably wiser answers to dilemmas like the Meaning of Life Problem, as follows: "In reflecting over their lives, people sometimes realize that they have not achieved what they had once planned to achieve. What should one/they do and consider?" So next time you're in need of an instant, small boost of wisdom, take a minute and just *imagine* chatting with a trusted partner or visiting other cultures.

EXERCISE 35
MORAL REASONING

In 2001, Baltes's frequent collaborator Ursula Staudinger proved what you might already suspect: moral reasoning and wisdom are linked. Specifically (and this is kind of cool albeit technical), for those who possess strong moral reasoning, wisdom increases with age. If you have lower moral reasoning, you gain no wisdom as you get older. So if you want wisdom later, train your moral reasoning now.

OK, so how do you train moral reasoning? Well, a slew of studies show that you can do it by thinking through moral dilemmas. Read the moral dilemmas below, write your well-reasoned answers, and then flip to the answers section of this book for discussion.

You're staying late at the law office where you work to finish a project and realize you've lost materials a coworker sent to you earlier in the week. You accidentally learned this coworker's e-mail password and so log on to her account to resend yourself the materials. But while on her account, you see she's been spending a good part of her workday playing Internet poker. Either ratting out your coworker to management or suggesting she curb her poker playing at work will require admitting you used her account, which is strictly verboten. What should you do?

Your friend Egbert just started an intimate relationship with the woman of his dreams. Unfortunately, unbeknownst to Egbert, the woman is your other friend Ronald's wife. Ronald, suspecting something, asks you for friendly counsel. Where does your loyalty lie? Whom should you crush? Or should you just stay quiet and hope it blows over?

Your spouse is sick and a drug will cure him/her. But you can't afford the drug. In this situation, is it justified to break into the laboratory of the drug manufacturer who sets the high price? Would it change the morality if the sick person were your child, your parent, or your dog instead of your spouse?

You are a conscripted soldier in a war you think is wrong and in which you've lost belief. Still, you love and respect your country and its laws of conscription. Are you right to go AWOL?

Your daughter was murdered, and while you're certain of who her killer is, there isn't enough evidence to convict him. You start spying on the killer in hopes of building a case. One of these spying evenings, the killer's wife is herself murdered and the killer you've been following is convicted of the crime. But you know he's innocent—you were watching him at the time of the crime. Is it your duty to offer an alibi?

An adult woman blames her parents' continuing iron-fisted control of her life for her indigence and substance-abuse problems. But when her parents *don't* watch over her, she spirals further into substance abuse. As her social worker, what would you counsel and why?

TEACH TO THE TESTS

How do you train wisdom? Well, if tests like the widely used SAWS, 3D-WS, and WDS *measure* wisdom, then activities that increase your scores on these tests *train* it. This was Robert Sternberg's reasoning when he designed a school curriculum around wisdom—he used the tests to break wisdom into its components and then trained each piece.

Below are components common to the SAWS, 3D-WS, and WDS tests, along with simple, life-based strategies to train them. Pick one a day until you've exhausted the list and then repeat as necessary.

1. **Don't take yourself so seriously:** Find at least one opportunity to laugh at yourself—bonus points for allowing others to laugh at you, too.

2. **Think about how the past affects the present and future:** Remember how a past event informs one of your present decisions or actions. Spend the day trying to recognize these present-to-past connections.

3. **Learn something new:** Ignorance may be bliss, but it's not wisdom—find an opportunity to learn about something completely foreign to you.

4. **Regulate your emotions:** Flip to this book's chapter on emotional intelligence and practice transforming your emotions to match the needs of situations.

5. **Find humor in the rough:** In Bill Cosby's wise words, "Once you find laughter, no matter how painful your situation might be, you can survive it." Nurture the wisdom of the Coz. Today, pick something difficult in your own life or in world events and find humor in it.

6. **Accept diversity:** Instead of summarily foreclosing on people who don't share your opinions, walk a proverbial mile in their shoes. Today, have a constructive conversation with a family member or Facebook friend who doesn't share your political views.

7. **Be curious:** It's easy to get stuck in the rut of cooking chicken with peppers while listening to classic rock. Instead, wisdom comes from curiosity—today, listen to new music, be it country, salsa, Stravinsky, or gamelan. And eat a new food—maybe check the ethnic aisle in the grocery store for something you've never seen before.

8. **Experience compassion:** Have a conversation today with someone who needs help. Chances are someone who fits the bill is all too easy to find. If not, search for online support groups and lend your compassionate voice to whatever chat you're most drawn to.

9. **Ask for help:** The wise know the limits of self-sufficiency. Look for an aspect of your life that's slipping through the cracks and ask for help. Do you need help keeping the house clean, saving money, enjoying life? Today's the day to get the help you need.

10. **Accept ambiguity:** Some problems have no answers. Spend today giving brainpower to one such intractable problem whose changing, contradictory, or ambiguous circumstances means there's no actual answer.

ANCIENT WISDOM VS. NONSENSE

This exercise is just for fun. Mostly. Just over half of the following sentences are ancient wisdom (or at least real quotes) and just fewer than half are nonsense from a range of random sentence generators.

Sort the wisdom from the nonsense. And then before you look at the answers to see which is really which, try to interpret the phrases you labeled wisdom. What do you think makes something "wise"?

The gleaming darkness confounds the fault.

When torrential water tosses boulders, it is because of its momentum.

A thesis presupposes the waste of this gleaming sky.

This thaw took a while to thaw; it's going to take a while to unthaw.

A dream presupposes wisdom: it is the immanent decision.

High-five is a skin ballot.

All you need is ignorance and confidence and then success is sure.

Our thinking and our behavior are always in anticipation of a response.

Any light cannot be the charm of our omnipotent passage.

I know the joy of fishes in the river through my own joy, as I go walking along the same river.

Ignorance is enhanced by the prudence of the benevolent thought.

The physical world, including our bodies, is a response of the observer.

The pure thought falsifies any passion.

Should a bass frown at an insult?

A wheel clicks before a sniff.

The poet extends into the rabbit.

One of the things important about history is to remember the true history.

Swift as the wind, quiet as the forest, conquer like the fire, steady as the mountain.

Pretend inferiority and encourage his arrogance.

Some divisibility reveals the passion of any original void.

The idea of the hidden performs the epistemology of unsituated knowledge.

Where can I find a man who has forgotten words so I can have a word with him?

The baster makes a good chicken nervous.

A frog in a well cannot conceive of the ocean.

One moon shows in every pool in every pool the one moon.

In theory there is no difference between theory and practice. In practice there is.

A man who carries a cat by the tail learns something he can learn in no other way.

Any universal thought destroys the spirit, which is the brilliant totality.

Any fertile vision is balanced by passion.

Civilization is the limitless multiplication of unnecessary necessities.

SELFISH SELFLESSNESS

Wisdom requires thought and action without yourself in mind, and sociologist Monika Ardelt of the University of Florida shows that selflessness is also the best predictor of successful aging. In fact, the wisdom born of selflessness beats out physical health, income, socioeconomic status, physical environment, and even social relationships in predicting life satisfaction in old age. Ultimately, selflessness has selfish outcomes.

WHY SMART PEOPLE DO DUMB THINGS

Robert Sternberg points to four fallacies that may make highly intelligent people even less likely *than people of average intelligence to develop wisdom. First is* egocentrism. *Smart people may be prone to thinking the world revolves around them or should revolve around them. Second is* omniscience—"*the idea that you know all there is to know and so don't need the counsel of others,*" *Sternberg says. Then there's the left hand of omniscience,* omnipotence. *As in theologian Reinhold Niebuhr's famous Serenity Prayer, wise people have the serenity to accept the things they know they can't change, whereas intelligent people are prone to thinking they can change everything. Finally, Sternberg adds* invulnerability *to the factors that can make intelligent people unwise. Within the armor of intelligence, unwise choices won't lead to unfortunate outcomes, right?*

CHAPTER 11

PERFORMANCE UNDER PRESSURE

The initial chip leader at the final table of the 2009 World Series of Poker Main Event was Darvin Moon, self-employed logger from Oakland, Maryland. Moon had won his entry ticket to the event on his third try at a $130-buy-in satellite tournament in Wheeling, West Virginia. The trip to Vegas for the WSOP was his first flight in a commercial airplane.

Sitting across from Moon was Steve Begleiter, a senior executive at the investment bank Bear Stearns, but a relative guppy at the WSOP final table, with 25 million chips to Moon's 58.6 million. Moon was dealt king, queen off-suit and made a reasonable raise to 1.3 million chips. Begleiter raised to 3.9 million and with everyone else folding, Moon, already invested in the pot, called. Then with a 2, 3, and 4 on the flop, Darvin Moon was left looking at a whole lot of nothing. He checked. Begleiter bet 5.35 million. With nothing but king-high, Moon eyed his cards and raised to 15 million—what the ESPN analyst described as "going fishing without a license." Begleiter licked his lips, swallowed, and pushed his chips—all in.

Now, being caught fishing without a license is one thing, but at that point Darvin Moon already had his line in the water to the tune of 15 million chips. It would've taken him only 6 million more chips to call for a chance not only at a pot worth 44.75 million chips but a chance to eliminate one of seven remaining players at the table. It's a call everyone at the final table makes with their eyes closed—that is, perhaps, with $6 and not $6 million on the line.

Darvin Moon folded. Analysts called it the worst fold in the history of tournament poker. Not only did Moon fold in the literal poker meaning of the word, but he folded in the sense of the collapse of his brain under pressure. Though Moon would go on to eliminate Begleiter, he'd lost the chip lead and ended up losing the tournament to twenty-one-year-old wunderkind Joe Cada.

By looking inside Darvin Moon's brain as it crumpled like a Coke can, you can learn to avoid similar mistakes.

First, while pressure seems like an esoteric, intangible thing, that's not the case in the brain. Instead it sits like a lead weight in your working memory, claiming space that could otherwise hold useful information. And because working memory is a mainline to general intelligence, space claimed by pressure makes you measurably dumber—you literally have less IQ in the face of a $6 million bet than you do in the face of a $6 one.

Interestingly, this leads to a nasty catch-22 for minorities—a recent study by University of Chicago researcher Sian Beilock, author of the book *Choke*, showed that a common worry of people from ethnic minorities when taking tests is that they might do poorly, and so confirm the negative stereotype of their minority—a worry that test-takers from the majority ethnicity don't share. According to Beilock, this unequal worry, called stereotype threat, claims space in working memory, making minorities score lower on the test and, cruelly, ensuring minorities confirm precisely the negative stereotype they'd been so worried about.

Add to reduced working-memory capacity what Beilock calls analysis paralysis: pressure flips a mental switch from implicit to explicit thought, making you apply a layer of analysis to things that should be automatic. It's as if when your mind recognizes a serious situation, it turns off the autopilot in favor of manual steering—only, it does so even in cases in which you've trained autopilot to be the better driver. It's very Zen: you can't think your way to performance under pressure, and the harder you try, the more likely you are to fail.

Your brain, cruelly forced by pressure to rely on analysis that's momentarily absent, responds by desperately trying to latch onto anything it considers an immediate win. On the scale of risk-versus-reward on which we base many of our decisions, pressure thumbs the scale on the side of perceived reward, making you prioritize risky choices with immediate payouts. For example, researchers Mara Mather and Nichole Lighthall showed that when subjects stuck their hands in ice water, the stress primed their brains' dopamine pumps to release more happy juice—meaning that under stressful conditions, a small reward creates the pleasure of a much larger reward. Likewise, chronic pressure can make you chronically prioritize the quick rewards of drugs and alcohol while discounting their long-term risk.

You can see this in a 1980 documentary film by researchers J. Zucker, D. Zucker, J. Abrahams, K. Abdul-Jabbar, et al, published under the title *Airplane!* In this groundbreaking work, a participant who happens to be the supervisor of an air traffic control tower remarks (due to increasingly nonoptimal control of an inbound plane), "Looks like I picked the wrong week to quit drinking!" As airplane control further deteriorates and pressure on the control tower increases, the participant escalates, remarking, "Looks like I picked the wrong week to quit smoking!" Later he admits, "Looks like I picked the wrong week to stop sniffing glue!" and finally, as a crash starts to seem inevitable, "Looks like I picked the wrong week to quit amphetamines!"

In any case, the more you're forced to wrestle your risk/reward balance back to level, the harder it gets to keep doing so. For example, in February 2012, the *New York Times* told the story of a sixteen-year-old named Felix who was arrested for the murder of Antonio Ramirez in Oakland, California. In the proverbial white room with a bare, swinging lightbulb, police pressed for a confession that Felix didn't want to give. When Felix finally started "cooperating," the police interrogators fed him details that helped him "remember" elements of the crime scene. Finally, late that night, the police taped Felix's confession. Three days later, when Felix was handed the charge sheet in court, he realized something kind of important: at the time of the murder, he'd been locked up in a juvenile detention facility for violating parole in an unrelated case. Under pressure, Felix's need for the immediate reward of relief outweighed the long-term consequences of confession.

So beware. Stress plugs your working memory, analysis paralysis forces you to try to use it anyway, and your dopamine circuits cry for a quick, risky solution. This nasty trio can lead to Darvin-Moon–like folding your way out of danger when it would've been wiser in the long term to call.

Now you're aware of the human tendency to punt under pressure, and this awareness alone can help bring you back to baseline decision-making under stress. Then, depending on the specific flavor of pressure, pick one of two opposite strategies to help you excel. Both strategies fight the plague of analysis paralysis, but from different directions. The difference, as hinted at above, is whether you've automated the best response. If you're facing a new stressful situation—one for which you don't have a strong, reliable instinctual response—your goal is to get past the burdens stress places on your working memory and apply meaningful analysis to the problem. If it's a familiar situation, your goal is to force your brain out of analysis so that your trained intuitions can stay in the mental driver's seat.

If you're facing a new form of pressure, a quartet of Greek researchers, including the colorfully named Antonis Hatzigeorgiadis, found that self-talk can help direct the needed analysis. This isn't the "I'm good enough, I'm smart enough, and doggone it, people like me!" of Stuart Smalley as played on *Saturday Night Live* by the (now) Democratic senator from Minnesota. Instead, it's instructional self-talk. Perhaps if you were defusing a bomb, it would be something along the lines of "First I cut the red wire, and then I gently slide out the detonation pin, and then ..." This instructional self-talk can divide a new, stressful task into seemingly more manageable components and focus your attention on each one in turn.

Then there are tasks you've automated, in which your goal should be to turn off that destructive layer of analysis that kicks in under pressure. Here, you'll want to apply a specific technique for silencing thought—turning what researcher Joan Vickers calls a quiet eye on the problem. In every sport she's studied, Vickers has identified crucial milliseconds that make or break the success of, for example, a free throw or putt or rifle shot or dart throw. And for each sport, there's a crucial point in space—the front of a basketball rim or the back of a golf ball. And across all sports, spending these milliseconds focused on the crucial point in space leads to success—swish, drain, bang, or bull's-eye.

By applying the quiet eye technique to her employer's women's basketball team at the University of Calgary, Vickers helped the Lady Dinos improve their free-throw shooting by 22 percent over two seasons and jump from a dismal seventeenth in their league to an astounding second in Canada. A similar study at Florida State of quiet eye in pool players found that focus on the cue ball and target ball without a lot of switching between the two was a major distinction between novice and expert players.

So the technique for executing a task you've done a thousand times before is this: ready, imagine, focus, execute, and evaluate. When you execute, do it quickly and smoothly, intentionally turning off the layer of analysis that creates paralysis.

Here's how it looks:

On June 4, 2012, playing the par-3 sixteenth hole at the PGA Memorial Golf Tournament in Dublin, Ohio, Tiger Woods hit his tee shot over the green and into an impossible lie in the rough, fifty feet away from the hole. As everyone in the civilized world knows, it had been a rough couple of years for Tiger, in which his personal life fell down a hole that suddenly his golf balls refused. Now, staring at a lightning-fast green sloping to water behind the hole, Woods could only lay up and hope to sink a tough par putt that would keep him a shot behind leader Rory Sabbatini.

Tiger stepped up to his demon lie, pulled a 60-degree wedge from his bag, and took a tentative-looking practice swing. ESPN said, "If he puts it short he's dead, if he puts it long he's dead."

In the forum for the Yahoo! News article describing Tiger's shot, a user named Thomas wrote, "I hit that shot with a 60° wedge last week and birdied hole 12 at a course here in Trumbull County. You can't beat that club for getting out of high grass." To which another user, Tom R, replied, "With all due respect, no, you didn't hit the same shot. No money on the line, no huge gallery following you, no pressure from 3 years of paying for your incredibly bad choices."

Like Darvin Moon at the WSOP final table, Tiger battled a working memory plugged with pressure, his brain screaming about the immediate reward of landing in the safe, close rough at the edge of the green.

Instead, he hit what Jack Nicklaus, whose record for career PGA wins Tiger hoped to tie at the tournament, called "the most unbelievable, gutsy shot I've ever seen." After his tentative practice swing, you can almost see Tiger tunneling through his mind, trying to find his intuition, doing an end run past working memory and its analytical failings. From fifty feet out, he landed his chip on the edge of the green, and on the ball's final revolution, it disappeared into the hole, turning the momentum of the tournament and perhaps his career. The difference between a hairless housecat and Tiger was all in his brain.

INTRINSIC VS. EXTRINSIC MOTIVATION

A 1997 summary of twenty-four studies shows that especially under pressure, people perform better when intrinsically motivated by the desire to master a task than when extrinsically motivated by rewards for peak performance. Many of these studies show that creating this difference is as easy as giving instructions that frame a task as an enjoyable challenge rather than a test. And the results hold true for pressure-filled tasks ranging from collage-making to creative writing to shooting basketball free throws to math to psychology tests to puzzles. So for a quick performance boost in pressure-filled situations, take a second to focus on the skill rather than the result. Work to improve and not necessarily to win and you'll win more often as a by-product.

COGNITIVE INTERVIEW

An extreme example of performance under pressure is the attempt of an eyewitness to recall the specifics of a violent event. A host of studies show that eyewitnesses tend to improve their memory of the violent event itself while losing memories of details surrounding the violence—a kind of tunnel vision so extreme that witnesses may lose important memories of faces and facts. Then there's been a ton of studies exploring how police interrogators can retrieve this lost information. You can use these strategies to retrieve your memories of stressful situations. And because remembering is a central component of learning, ensuring the accurate memory of, say, a heated boardroom argument, a fight with a significant other or child, or a high-stakes poker hand can help you learn to perform better the next time the situation arises. In fact, accurate memory of any stressful situation leads to better decisions and actions next time.

Think back to a stressful situation. Then remember its details by applying the following four basic pieces of a cognitive interview, as described in a 1996 paper in the *American Journal of Psychology* by UCLA psychologist Edward Geiselman:

1. **Reinstate the context:** Try to reinstate in your mind the context surrounding the incident. Think about what the surrounding environment looked like at the scene, such as rooms, the weather, and any nearby people or objects. Also think about how you were feeling at the time and think about your reactions to the incident.

2. **Report everything:** Some people hold back information because they are not quite sure that the information is important. Don't edit anything out of your report, even things you think may not be important.

3. **Recall the events in different order:** It's natural to go through the incident from beginning to end. However, you also should try to go through the events in reverse order. Or try starting with the thing that impressed you the most in the incident and then go from there, remembering both forward in time and backward.

4. **Change perspectives:** Try to recall the incident from different perspectives that you may have had, or adopt the perspectives of

others who were present during the incident. For example, try to place yourself in the role of a prominent character in the incident and think about what he or she must have seen.

COMBATTING EXPERT CHOKING

University of Chicago's Sian Beilock shows that expert golfers don't remember the minutiae of their putting strokes—they've trained putting to automaticity and so no longer store the specifics of their actions. Beilock calls this "expert-induced amnesia." She also shows this is an important reason why experts choke. See, pressure *forces* expert golfers to analyze their putting stroke, but when they look in their consciousness for these procedural specifics—Oh God!—the specifics are nowhere to be found. Instead, there's a very disturbing nothing.

Beilock also shows how to combat this tendency to choke under unavoidable and disturbing self-scrutiny: experts should store techniques not only in automaticity but in consciousness as well. She created this effect by videotaping putters during training, supposedly so that experts could later scrutinize their technique. Of course, knowing they'd be studied tricked golfers into analyzing their *own* technique during training, and they stored this analysis in consciousness. Now not only could they putt, but they knew *how* they putted—and Beilock showed they had effectively vaccinated themselves against choking. Whenever pressure forced analysis, they now had analysis in spades.

You can do the same thing. Think of something you've automated, be it cooking breakfast, driving, typing a fairly standardized e-mail, or shooting a free throw. Next time you're doing it, keep a running commentary of *how* you're doing *what* you're doing. Codify this procedure. Making your expert, unconscious behaviors conscious will allow you to find these behaviors in your brain when you need them most.

COMBATTING NOVICE CHOKING

Of course, experts aren't the only ones who choke. Novices choke too, but for very different reasons. Again, novices haven't made their behaviors automatic and so instead depend on working memory to guide them through tasks (oh, and some tasks—especially cognitive rather than motor tasks—you simply can't automate). These novices can't *feel* their way through and instead have to *think* their way through. And as we've seen, pressure claims space in working memory—it's as if under pressure, novices have to do two things at once: deal with pressure and deal with the task. And that's not just a metaphor: Sian Beilock showed that training novices under what's called a *dual-task condition* leads to better performance later, when pressure plays the role of a second task. Beilock did this by forcing subjects to monitor a string of words for a target word while learning to putt. You shouldn't have any trouble finding an equally distracting task. Whatever it is, combine the distraction with your training so that later, when pressure provides a distraction, your brain is already used to doing two things at once.

PRACTICE LIKE YOU PLAY
(SO YOU CAN PLAY LIKE YOU PRACTICE)

To create pressure, Beilock told her putters that if they could improve their performance by 20 percent over a final, pressure-filled eighteen putts they'd earn $5. The result: practicing under pressure led to better performance under pressure. So when practicing your own skill, it's useful to ratchet up the stakes. No one is likely to bet $5 on your practice, but here's how to create a similar kind of pressure: Pick the most egregious political cause you can think of. Search online for a way to donate to this cause and impose a $5 donation as a penalty for poor performance—consider penalizing yourself for lack of improvement. Now when you practice, there's something at stake—and when you perform, you'll be used to this pressure.

ANALYSIS PARALYSIS IN BASKETBALL

For forty-six minutes, professional basketball players generally shoot when they should shoot, pass when they should pass, and make overall good strategy decisions. And then come the final two minutes. You'd think that due to the importance of these final two minutes, players would buckle down and do the right thing, but the opposite is true. Especially when games are close, players' decision-making tanks toward the end, leading to a much higher rate of bad decisions in the form of desperately hopeful shots and stupid fouls.

Of course, the coach knows this is a critical time, so he draws up a detailed plan filled with X's and O's and dotted lines and covers it with a fine sheen of spittle as he explains exactly what to do in these pivotal seconds. And he thus further dooms players to overthink the final play, when they should be letting their highly trained instincts take over.

ANALYSIS PARALYSIS ON WIPEOUT

On the gladiatorial TV game show Wipeout, *hotties versus nerds edition, I took first-place finishes in the first two obstacle courses into the semifinals. In that round was an element that required jumping from a platform onto a spinning bar, riding it to another platform, and then jumping off. Only, the landing platform was soap-slick, tiny, and twenty feet above the water. I was first to the obstacle, hopped atop the spinning bar, slid off, and* nearly *caught the handle on the landing platform, but instead slid off and took the plunge. I did it again. And again. And as I*

*slid off the landing platform for the umpteenth time, I watched first one
and then two and finally three competitors pass me and claim the spots
in the finals.*

*It turned out I'd been doing it wrong. Had I simply hung from the
spinning bar instead of riding atop it, it would have draped me softly
across the landing platform. Instead, I crashed onto it from above with
a momentum I couldn't control. Blame it on analysis paralysis. I over-
thought the obstacle with a plugged working memory, leading to the
wrong solution. And then I stuck with it even once the intuition of my
body screamed time and again it was the wrong way—all the way to the
death knell of the final foghorn.*

CHAPTER 12

EMOTIONAL INTELLIGENCE

"There's an old graph about empathy and sales performance," says John (Jack) Mayer, University of New Hampshire professor and one of the pioneers of emotional intelligence research. "*Some* empathy is good—being clueless isn't helpful. But then too much empathy is bad. It hurts sales."

Mayer saw this firsthand during two years between college and grad school when he had a gig as a writer/researcher studying car sales managers in Michigan. He remembers that "in some dealerships, the most outperforming salespeople would be there gagging with laughter over having sold some poor person a clunker for $500 over invoice." These salespeople had enough empathy to connect with the customer and make the sale—but not so much that it bothered them to rip someone off.

In Mayer's research on emotional intelligence, he identified four factors that seemed central to the way humans experience and use emotions: perceiving emotions, reasoning with emotions as a piece of the decision puzzle, understanding emotions and being able to verbalize them, and being able to appropriately and effectively manage emotions.

"We saw that emotions are like chess pieces," says Mayer, "and each moves in its idiosyncratic way. Anger has its moves; happiness and love have their own moves. People who recognize, reason with, understand, and manage these emotions can play the game."

To see if facility with this piece-pushing has any real-world purpose, Mayer, his grad student at the time Marc Brackett, and Rebecca Warner asked people to fill out a 1,500-item survey that included "everything from what's in the fridge to what clubs they belong to, to how many pictures they have on the mantel," he says. And then he and his colleagues tried to discover which factors on these surveys pointed toward outcomes representative of strong emotional kung fu, such as less drug abuse, less fighting and arguments, more contact with parents, how someone is perceived in the workplace, and so on.

Sure enough, they were able to show, for example, that students with high emotional intelligence (EI) have lower rates of drug use and teachers with high EI get more support from their principals. Employees with high EI have higher job performance, especially when their IQ is low (implying that emotional intelligence can help compensate for low general intelligence—and also that these skills are distinct). EI is even implicated in resilience—the more EI you have, the higher your chances of bouncing back after trauma or negative life events.

So which is it? Like empathy in car salesmen, is there an optimal degree of emotional intelligence or is more EI simply better?

Mayer's former grad student Marc Brackett—who now happens to be director of the Yale Center for Emotional Intelligence—solved this seeming paradox, illustrating his explanation with a story about his own experience in the stock market. "I'm obsessive-compulsive about my stocks," he says, "but I don't buy and sell every day, because I'm aware that it's a game for me and I don't actually allow myself to do stupid things." The difference between Brackett and Wall Street traders whom many studies show are led by their emotional noses into imprudent trades is that, while Brackett and these traders both experience emotions powerfully, Brackett overlays these emotions with the understanding that he needn't act on them.

And according to Jack Mayer, this combination of being able to both recognize and manage emotions is precisely what makes up the best EI: "intuition overlain with reason—both the visceral experience of emotion and the cerebral ability to direct it." This is the difference between the useful and the detrimental experience of emotion: If you can't reason with emotions, to a large degree you're better off being oblivious to them.

For example, imagine you're feeling insecure in a meeting. If you're unaware of this insecurity, you simply act like that idiot we all know, laughing at inappropriate times, stepping on toes, boasting or mumbling, and generally making an ass of yourself. Now imagine you're aware of your insecurity but unable to regulate it. It's even worse— like watching your life train-wreck in super slow motion. But if you can overlay emotional perception with emotional logic, you can learn to manage and even control this insecurity and thereby avoid looking like an ass.

To accomplish this, Marc Brackett recommends an approach similar to becoming a ninja. Seriously. "My other career is teaching martial arts," Brackett says, "and you're required to learn different skills to earn different-colored belts, different ranks." Start simply, he says, learning to recognize the seven basic emotions of anger, fear, disgust, contempt, joy, sadness, and surprise. Then progress to understanding, labeling, expressing, and regulating these emotions. Brackett names these steps according to the acronym RULER.

The last step, regulating, is the difference between using emotions and being irrationally led by them. It's what keeps Brackett from day trading and would allow the underperforming car salesman to decide whether or not to act on his empathy.

Of course, emotions don't always require redirection. Maybe after overlaying intuition with analysis, you still feel like a stock trade is a smart choice—using analysis to validate useful emotions can be as powerful as using it to regulate away useless ones.

So the answer to whether it's best to recognize emotions or live blissfully unaware of them is this: if you can't put the final "R" on RULER, you might as well not put on the first. But if you can both be sensitive to emotions and control them, you have a powerful tool in navigating the emotional landscape of life.

EXERCISE 43
RECOGNIZING AND LABELING EMOTIONS

As part of their EI training intended for businesses and schools, researchers Andrew Morris and his colleagues use art to train emotional recognition and labeling—the first "R" and "L" in Marc Brackett's RULER. (Though their list of basic emotions doesn't exactly match Brackett's.) They note that in one study, this training incidentally led to a 30 percent increase in community service hours in those trained. Here's how it works:

Do a quick Google image search for the term "portraits" or "portrait." Then read the list of emotions below and pick the best emotions to label the faces you see. Then (and this is important!) list the non-verbal clues you used to reach your answers. This training matches Marc Brackett's description of making the implicit learning of emotion explicit—not just knowing, but dissecting *how* you know.

Once you've mastered portraits, try it with abstract art and poems (you could use the poetry archives at the *New Yorker, Atlantic,* and thedailyverse.com). Then try it with music.

EMOTIONS:

Anger: fury, outrage, resentment, wrath, exasperation, animosity, annoyance, irritability, hostility, hatred

Sadness: grief, sorrow, gloom, melancholy, self-pity, loneliness, dejection, despair

Fear: anxiety, apprehension, nervousness, concern, consternation, misgiving, wariness, qualm, edginess, dread, fright, terror, panic

Disgust: contempt, disdain, scorn, abhorrence, aversion, distaste, revulsion

Shame: guilt, embarrassment, chagrin, remorse, humiliation, regret, mortification

Enjoyment: happiness, joy, relief, contentment, bliss, delight, amusement, pride, thrill, rapture, sensual pleasure, gratification, satisfaction, euphoria, whimsy, ecstasy

Love: acceptance, friendliness, trust, kindness, affinity, devotion, adoration, infatuation

Surprise: shock, astonishment, amazement, wonder

EXERCISE 44
UNDERSTANDING EMOTIONS

Children quickly develop what are called *first-order beliefs*—the ability to infer what someone else is thinking. For example, a child might say of a begging Labrador that "the dog wants a treat." Trickier are *second-order beliefs*—knowing what someone thinks someone else is thinking. For example, explaining that a storybook character gave a dog a treat because the character knew the dog wanted it. This is emotional understanding. It's also the distinction between a lie and a joke. For example, in a study of autistic children's ability to distinguish lies from jokes, psychologists Susan Leekam and Margot Prior point out that "the ability to distinguish a lie from a joke involves deciding whether a person *wants* to be believed." And sure enough, people with low emotional intelligence, as is generally the case in those with autism spectrum disorders, have a tough time sorting the jokers from the liars.

Working through this distinction can help you improve your ability to understand emotion—the "U" in Marc Brackett's RULER. The following stories present instances of lying or joking. Your job is not only to distinguish the two but to justify your answers in the language of second-order beliefs—what do the characters in these stories think the other characters believe? How does one character's intention to be believed or disbelieved make the distinction between a lie and a joke? Don't look in the back of the book—the answers aren't there. Instead, the process of reasoning through these on your own whether you're technically right or wrong is what will improve your ability to understand emotions in your own life.

> After returning from the community rec center, a six-year-old tells his father that he finally summoned the courage to go down the large, yellow twisty slide into the water. He didn't actually go down the slide.
>
> A coworker asks if you parked in the Employee of the Month spot. You say no, it's not your car. But it is.
>
> A coworker asks if you parked in the Employee of the Month spot. He's the employee of the month. You say no, it's not your car. But you know that he knows that it is.
>
> A dad tells his kids the bath is ready—the perfect temperature!—but when the first kid hops in, he's surprised to find it ice cold.
>
> Your nervous Labrador leaves a steaming pile in a hidden corner of the veterinarian's office. When the receptionist asks whose

dog is responsible, you don't say anything, but you know she probably suspects you.

Your neighbor wonders if perhaps your Labrador snuck into his yard and ate the largest koi from his backyard pond. Having just buried in your own backyard the mostly-eaten remains of said koi, you say no—of course your dog didn't eat the fish.

A four-year-old tells her father that Templeton, the pet guinea pig, has escaped. When Dad looks, there's Templeton still sitting in the cage. The girl says that must be a new guinea pig and not Templeton.

Your mother-in-law wonders if you know anything about the whereabouts of her teeth? You disavow all knowledge. In fact, you've inserted them into the motion-activated singing bass over the fireplace, which she gave you for Christmas. You hope your wife notices later and not your mother-in-law now.

All three of the new pet fish, named after Disney princesses, are dead. You surreptitiously replace them with live look-alikes. When the kids notice the fish have slightly changed color, you blame it on water temperature. Everyone is mollified, but you think they suspect the truth.

A friend says you've got to meet this guy/girl he knows—you'd, like, *totally* hit it off! But the date turns out to be the friend's somewhat odd brother/sister.

A four-year-old points and yells, "Spider on your shirt!" You jump six feet in the air. There is no spider.

A husband tells his wife that of course he remembered to turn off the sprinkler like she asked before they left the house. He says that he's forgotten his wallet and while "retrieving" it from home, turns off the sprinkler.

Two kids are terrified of a tiny black spider that's run under the edge of a carpet. The father says he knows where it is—under a specific corner. With trepidation, the kids get ready to lift the corner. The father has sneakily placed a gigantic rubber tarantula under this corner.

EXPRESSING EMOTIONS

Now on to the "E" in RULER: expressing emotions. Successful emotional expression matches emotion to situation. For example, if you're looking forward to a reward, the most reasonable emotion to feel would be hope, whereas once the reward is actually present, the appropriate emotion is joy. If the same were true of a future/current *punishment,* you might feel trepidation and then distress. Generally, there are five characteristics of situations that work together to determine the "correct" emotion: motivational state (are you avoiding something bad or seeking something good?), situational state (is the good or bad thing predicted or actually present?), probability (is the outcome certain or uncertain?), legitimacy (do you deserve the outcome?), and agency (is the situation caused by circumstance, others, or yourself?).

A 1990 study by Ira Roseman asked participants to pick apart these five factors. Basically, Roseman had participants recall an experience of joy and then one of relief, or affection and then pride, or sadness and then fear—and then had participants rate these emotions according to the five factors. Consensus over 161 subjects showed which emotions match which situations. For a massive table of results, search online for "Appraisals of Emotion-Eliciting Events," but, for one example of many, they found that the emotion of disgust has high legitimacy (it's deserved) whereas shame does not.

Following are the pairs of emotions that Roseman and his colleagues used in their study, along with a couple more recommended by Marc Brackett. For each emotion, write the memory of an experience when you felt it. Once you've finished listing experiences, revisit these experiences to discover what, exactly, makes you feel, for example, regret rather than guilt, or joy rather than relief. If you're up for it, use the language of the five characteristics of emotional situations to describe the motivational state, situational state, probability, legitimacy, and agency of your emotional experiences. This exercise is a bit tricky but will boost your ability to express situationally appropriate emotions.

Here are the paired emotions:

Joy	Relief

Affection	Pride

Hope	Surprise

Disgust	Distress

Sadness	Fear

Unfriendliness	Anger

Frustration	Shame

Regret	Guilt

Envy	Jealousy

Pity	Sympathy

REGULATING EMOTION

Last but not least, the all-important final "R" in Brackett's RULER! A 1996 study found more than two hundred ways to regulate emotion, including exercise, venting, drinking, and seeking social support. Luckily, Stanford's James Gross boils it down to the following five major categories of emotional self-regulation strategies. For each, learn about the strategy and then list ways in which the strategy does or could apply to your life.

SITUATION SELECTION
Approaching or avoiding people, places, and things to regulate emotion. For example, staying away from the racetrack or seeking out a good friend. Beware overbalancing the short-term gains of avoiding an

emotionally stressful situation with long-term losses. For example, a shy person who avoids parties may further lose the ability to socialize.

Exercise: List a situation that you find emotionally challenging and then another that is emotionally recharging:

_____

_____

_____

SITUATION MODIFICATION

For example, a flat tire on the way to an important meeting is crazy-making until you decide to make it a conference call. Researchers call this *problem-focused coping.* This can be internal as well as external—for example, you could change the meeting to a conference call (external) or you could just decide it's not so important after all (internal).

Exercise: How have you sculpted a situation's emotion? List one time you got needlessly worked up and one time you made the best of a bad thing:

_____

_____

_____

SELECTIVE ATTENTION

This falls into the three subcategories of *distraction, concentration,* and *rumination.* Distraction can be focusing on ceiling tiles or on that proverbial happy place in your heart and mind. Concentration is blotting out emotion with an all-consuming activity, be it thinking about your garden or actually gardening. And rumination focuses attention on emotions themselves and their consequences rather than fixating on the situations that cause them, though it's the most fraught of the three because rumination on sadness can lead to depression and rumination on negative consequences of emotion can lead to anxiety about expressing them.

Exercise: List one distraction and one thing you can concentrate on to regulate your emotion:

_____

_____

_____

COGNITIVE CHANGE

You can choose the personal meaning you attach to a situation or reframe a situation to transform the emotion it elicits. For example, you might reframe an exam as an opportunity to improve rather than a high-stakes test of your personal worth. Or you can reappraise failure in light of a task's partial successes. Or you can compare yourself to those less fortunate.

Exercise: Pick a situation that makes you feel bad or anxious or stressed out. How could you reframe this situation in a positive light?

_____

_____

_____

RESPONSE MODULATION

This includes regulating an emotion itself through psychiatric drugs, relaxation strategies, or the like, and also exerting control over the expression of the emotion. Some people call this second step *repression,* and it can have negative consequences, as seen in studies showing that inhibiting the expression of emotion actually makes you feel the bad aspects of it more keenly.

Exercise: List a situation in which you tend to repress emotion. Now list a situation in which you think you could and should show *more* emotion:

_____

_____

_____

|||||||||||||||||||||||||||||||||||||||| **EXERCISE 47** ||||||||||||||||||||||||||||||||||||||||
WORDS AND MEANING

Chris Argyris of the Harvard Business School has a nice technique for training people to understand the hidden meanings of speech, but it takes a partner and some work. With your partner, record and transcribe a meaningful conversation (or have Google Voice transcribe the recording for you). Make a copy of the transcript for yourself and another for your partner. Note in the margins what you were thinking while you were speaking and also note what you think the other person meant but didn't say. Have your partner do it, too. Then compare notes—how close were your interpretations to your partner's intended meanings? Argyris uses this exercise to highlight the disconnect between words and thoughts—both the small and large dishonesties in our own speech and the implicit assumptions that we make when listening.

EMOTIONALLY DISTURBED (OR SIMPLY UNAWARE)

"My niece is six and goes to a high-level school in Princeton, New Jersey," says Marc Brackett. The school implemented an emotional literacy program and Brackett describes asking his niece if he could peek at her feelings book, "because, you know, it's kind of Uncle Marc's thing, honey." She was happy to show Uncle Marc, who was horrified to find that she'd circled 10 on a scale of 1 to 10 describing her level of anxiety. "I thought, Oh my God, my little niece is experiencing anxiety disorder!" Brackett says. He realized it was his duty to counsel her, and readied his emotional crisis intervention strategies. But in the course of superheroism, he realized his niece had absolutely no clue what "anxiety" meant. She didn't have anxiety disorder, she'd simply been asked to jump to brown-belt emotional skills before earning her yellow belt.

EMOTIONS TRUMP REASON

Emotions may be clogging Congress, sinking the economy, and killing polar bears. "We decide based on feelings, not facts," says Paul Slovic, founder of the Decision Research Center in Eugene, Oregon, and past president of the Society for Risk Analysis. When it comes to emotionally charged subjects like climate change, "scientific evidence and argument bounce off them like bullets off the 'S' on Superman's chest," he says.

CHAPTER 13

WILLPOWER

If IQ is the strength of the bulb in your lighthouse, willpower is the lens that focuses it into a beam. "What's really fundamental to performance is the ability to control the objects of our attention. To choose what information our mind is going to work on and buffer it from sources of distraction. It's the ability to keep some things in mind and keep other information out," says Temple University neuroscientist Jason Chein.

Willpower is also the subject of a very good book of the same name by *New York Times* columnist John Tierney and his collaborator, famed psychologist Roy Baumeister. Their storyline of a finite pool of willpower explains, for example, why less financially secure shoppers are more likely to buy candy in the checkout line. See, the grocery store is filled with temptations and trade-offs in which you spend not only money but your reserve of willpower. While using willpower to inhibit the urge to splurge on delicious unhealthy treats like cream-filled doughnuts and Ruffles potato chips, you're also making difficult financial decisions like whether it's worth $4.29 for a loaf of bakery multigrain bread when you can get a long loaf of store-brand wheat bread for $1.99, or weighing the cost/benefit of genuine Vermont maple syrup. The less money you have, the more important and difficult these financial decisions are. The more difficult these decisions are, the more willpower you burn while making them—and the less you have remaining to fend off Reese's Peanut Butter Cups at the checkout stand. Voilà: poor people spend more on checkout candy.

Tierney and Baumeister point to a biological cause of this wearing down of our inhibitory powers: willpower costs glucose, and eventually we run low. In a 2007 review for the journal *Personality and Social Psychology,* Baumeister wrote that "numerous self-control behaviors fit this pattern [of glucose-dependent willpower], including controlling attention, regulating emotions, quitting smoking, coping with stress, resisting impulsivity, and refraining from criminal and aggressive behavior." In the lab, Baumeister showed that as you make decisions, your brain glucose decreases, that people with lower blood glucose show less willpower, and that when you hit people with the sugary lab equivalent of a Slurpee, you can reinvigorate willpower.

But there's another theory of willpower endurance that doesn't depend on simple sugars. Carol Dweck and Greg Walton believe it's, well, all in your head. They put subjects through a brain-draining regimen similar to the Baumeister tests—asking half of their subjects to do something automatic like cross off all the e's (and E's) in a page of text and the other half to cross off e's according to a tricky set of willpower-sucking rules. Then everyone did another test. As you'd expect, on the whole the fresh group did better on this second test than the drained group. But there was a split in the drained group, with some of these depleted subjects doing just as well as the fresh ones. It turned out the secret of these willpower-endurance champions was something very simple: they believed that their well of willpower was bottomless. In their minds, willpower wasn't a limited resource but rather something you could call upon endlessly, if you just dug a little deeper. And like the Baumeister experiments, Dweck's work jumps the lab. She followed 153 college students through final exam week and found that the students who saw willpower as an unlimited resource ate less junk food, procrastinated less, and, as you might expect, ultimately earned better grades than students who believed their willpower could simply run out. Then, like giving subjects a sugar drink, when Dweck and her colleagues helped students believe in unlimited willpower, they saw willpower itself increase. Writing in the *New York Times,* Dweck explained her work, saying, "People who think that willpower is limited are on the lookout for signs of fatigue. When they detect fatigue, they slack off. People who get the message that willpower is not so limited may feel tired, but for them this is no sign to give up—it's a sign to dig deeper and find more resources."

To Dweck, it's not necessarily sugar we need but a swift kick in the cerebral pants. Believe that you always have more willpower in the tank and you will have more willpower in the tank.

So there it is—an overview of the two major schools of thought on willpower, along with two compelling ways to boost it: a sugary drink, or belief there's more to be found. Following are a couple more tips that can help you find the willpower you need.

EXERCISE 48
NEURAL REPROCESSING

University of Minnesota psychologist Philip Zelazo uses the famous marshmallow experiment to describe another way to boost willpower—do you eat one marshmallow now or can you inhibit that urge for twenty minutes in order to earn a second? "You have the urge to eat," Zelazo says, "and then the information is fed forward into parts of the prefrontal cortex, which returns it back into the system for another iteration of processing."

Elsewhere we've looked at decisions as a want/should teeter-totter, but in Zelazo's model it's more like a tennis match—the urge serves, the prefrontal cortex returns, and then the two rally. The more attention you give to the prefrontal side of the court, the more chance willpower will eventually win.

"Your reprocessing might look like 'Wow, that marshmallow sure looks tasty, but now I'm starting to pay attention to the long-term reward of waiting.' Next time through processing, you can amplify attention to that long-term reward even more," Zelazo says. He calls this state of intentional reprocessing *mindfulness,* though other researchers might call it expressing high willpower.

"The more you engage in that practice of stopping and reflecting, the easier it gets. You're literally growing your prefrontal cortex," Zelazo says.

He also describes this mindful reprocessing as allowing a deeper experience of the present, not only in terms of noticing more, but also in noticing your own reactions to situations. For example, you might think, "I find this feature interesting, I wonder why? You can elaborate your cognitive processing of this situation so that you not only respond directly to the environment but modulate and modify your own subjective and cognitive experiences. If you practice being mindful in a range of situations through the day, then that becomes your mode of experiencing," Zelazo says.

So try being mindful. You can do it now or you can practice in your cognitive downtime. Notice your surroundings. This part is hard enough: does your attention slide to your e-mail or your shopping list or other things outside the present? Once you're successfully centered, also notice what you're noticing. Why does your attention rest where it rests? What does the natural center of your attention make you feel? And then, importantly, shift around this attention and experiment with multiple interpretations of where it rests.

"Simply by the act of neural reprocessing, you become better at neural reprocessing," Zelazo says.

GRAMMATICAL REASONING

In 1968, famed psychologist Alan Baddeley showed that you could measure scuba divers' cognitive function (and thus diagnose nitrogen narcosis) with a three-minute test of grammatical reasoning. His test has since been used to explore cognitive effects of, for example, sleep deprivation, altitude, a good breakfast, and the unawareness of one's own incompetence. The many neat effects found with the grammatical reasoning test include the finding that a quick pass through the test primes subjects to apply reason to situations in their own lives—right away, you can use a couple of the following slips to prime your brain for reason! But too much of the test results in cognitive fatigue and *worse* performance on life tasks—that is, unless you build up your tolerance. It takes willpower to conquer cognitive fatigue.

HOW TO BUILD IT

First copy and cut out the following slips. As you can see, they're in the form of, for example, "A precedes B—AB." Unless you've been more than thirty meters underwater for quite some time, you can tell this example is true. But many sentences are false. Your job is to distinguish true from false as quickly as possible. Stack the slips, shuffle them, and flip them one at a time—despite the fact that every slip is easy, it takes disciplined reason to pass through the entire deck without error. (If you like, write "true" or "false" on the back of each slip for easy checking.) Write down your time, adding ten seconds for each error. Then come back to the grammatical reasoning test to periodically check for improvement. As you practice, your ability to make it through this grammatical reasoning test without error should increase.

A precedes B—AB	A precedes B—BA
B precedes A—AB	B precedes A—BA
A does not precede B—AB	A does not precede B—BA
B does not precede A—AB	B does not precede A—BA
A follows B—AB	A follows B—BA
B follows A—AB	B follows A—BA
A does not follow B—AB	A does not follow B—BA
B does not follow A—AB	B does not follow A—BA
A comes after B—AB	A comes after B—BA
B comes after A—AB	B comes after A—BA
A does not come after B—AB	A does not come after B—BA
B does not come after A—AB	B does not come after A—BA

PAIRED ASSOCIATES

Along with working memory and task switching, willpower is an important component of *executive function*—our ability to control our *attention* and plan with *intention*. This version of the paired associates task trains working memory, along with the willpower needed to inhibit the distraction of a previous rule (don't worry: this will make sense in a second). Virginia Rosen of the National Institute of Mental Health showed that once you struggle to cram a rule into your working memory, it takes considerable willpower to rewrite that rule in later trials. Rosen also shows that people who train this skill experience fewer unwanted intrusions on their thoughts—in other words, this exercise trains the focus and inhibition components of the willpower you bring to life.

Here's a version of her exercise:

Shuffle a deck of playing cards. Draw two cards. These "associates" are now "paired." Remember the pairing. Write each card under the A and B columns of the TRAIN section of the first chart on page 168. For example, if you'd drawn Queen of Spades and the 7 of Clubs, you would write Q-Spade and 7-Clubs under TRAIN. Set aside the card from the A column—you'll use it later. Make four total pairs of associates this way, recording their letters in the A/B TRAIN columns as you did for the first pair. Each time, set aside the "A column" card as you did for the first pair, so that once you're done you have four "A column" cards remaining.

Now cover the TRAIN column of the chart and switch to the TEST column. Pick a card from your short deck of A's. List the card and then try to remember the associate card you paired with it. For example, if you drew the Queen of Spades, the proper response would be 7 of Clubs. One at a time, flip over all cards from your little A deck and re-member/list their associates. Then reveal the TRAIN column to check your answers.

This should be relatively easy. Don't worry: it gets harder.

So far, this has been a working-memory exercise. Now it becomes a test of willpower. Pick new associates for your "A" cards—on the second chart, list the same cards in the A column and draw new cards to list in the C column. You now have new responses (C) for your stimuli (A). Now when you test your recall of these paired associates as before, not only must you flex your working memory to recall the pairings, but you must flex your willpower to inhibit the previous pairings.

Check your answers. If you got any wrong, repeat the exercise from the beginning with completely new pairs of associates. If you were perfect, boost the difficulty by sketching your own TRAIN/TEST chart with five blank rows and adding a fifth pair of associates. You can also run further trials with the same "A" cards—you paired A-B and A-C, now continue to pair A with D, and even A with E, choosing ever-evolving responses to pair with your stimuli cards. Adding more pairs or continuing to pair stimuli with new responses will train your ability to keep in mind the information you want and push aside the information you don't.

Train		Test	
A	B	A	B

Train		Test	
A	C	A	C

Train		Test	
A	D	A	D

Train		Test	
A	E	A	E

EXERCISE 51
COUNT TO TEN

"One of the oldest ways to describe mindfulness is not just intending to do what you do, but super-intending it," Philip Zelazo says. "When you're walking, don't just walk and multitask, but experience that walking. Be present. Be where you are and be absorbed." Here's an exercise to practice this super-intention: Count to ten. Really, do it now. But as you count, don't think about anything other than counting. For me it goes something like this: "One, two ... I wonder what's in the fridge?" or "One, two, three ... gosh, I'm really doing it! D'oh!" Though seemingly simple, this may be the book's most difficult exercise—the willpower to inhibit distraction when not otherwise blunting it with a consuming task is horrifically difficult.

EXERCISE 52
AVOID TEMPTATION
(SO YOU DON'T HAVE TO RESIST IT)

Roy Baumeister and his colleagues did a nifty experiment: they gave subjects smartphones that beeped seven times a day. Each time one of the 205 participants' smartphones beeped, he or she noted whether they were feeling a desire, the nature and strength of the desire, whether the desire created internal conflict, and whether the subject was subsequently successful at resisting the desire. About half the time, subjects reported feeling desires, which included hunger (28 percent), sleep (10 percent), thirst (9 percent), sex (5 percent), and coffee (3 percent). When people attempted to resist desire, the desire won 17 percent of the time; when they didn't try to resist desire, they fulfilled it 70 percent of the time. It also turned out that some people were wildly more successful at resisting desire than others. What was it about these people? Was it Conan the Barbarian–esque willpower? No, in this study, it turned out the secret to resisting temptation was *lack of opportunity to consummate the desire*—it wasn't that people successfully inhibited the urge to drink a fourth cup of coffee, it was that the fourth cup of coffee didn't exist.

One powerful secret to resisting a temptation is to avoid situations where that temptation can easily be consummated. It's easy to see how you can put this to use in breaking yourself of bad habits in your own life. If you hate how much time you waste on the Internet when you should be working, don't just try to resist the urge to surf—instead consider using a program that stops you from going online during certain hours. If you're trying to break a videogame addiction, don't try to resist the siren call of your Xbox; instead unplug it from the TV, stick it in a box, and relegate it to the back of your coat closet.

EXERCISE 53
THE WELL OF WILLPOWER

Here's a version of the Carol Dweck and Gregory Walton task from this chapter that measures and trains willpower. As in the Paired Associates exercise, it consists of learning a rule and then using willpower to break it. Pick a text-heavy page in this book (or any other book you have lying around) and time yourself as you cross off every letter *e* (or letter *E*). Now flip to a similar text-heavy page and this time, cross off every *e, except those that are followed by another vowel*. Finally, flip to another page and again time yourself, this time crossing off every *e* except those that are *preceded* by another vowel. Now you've made one pass through this exercise—keep a log of your times. Tomorrow, do the same thing. As the difference in the times it takes you to apply these three *e*-crossing rules shrinks, your ability to inhibit distraction and maintain focus grows!

THE DUBIOUS AND DISTRACTING MOZART EFFECT

You know the line: listening to classical music, Mozart specifically, makes you better at anything else you're doing at the same time. But recent research shows that people who listen to music in the background as they work perform worse. The effect holds across all listener preferences and styles of music, and the reason is, as you might've guessed, willpower: background music is a distraction that you must spend precious willpower to inhibit, leaving you with less focus for the task at hand.

CHAPTER 14

MULTITASKING

Despite what you might've heard, there's actually no such thing as true multitasking. Imaging studies show your brain can only pay attention to one task at a time. But the *appearance* of multitasking is a central skill of most modern lives. How can the brain pull off the illusion of doing two, three, or fourteen things at once? The answer is what researchers call *task switching*—the ability to flip our attention so quickly and seamlessly from task to task and back again as necessary, monitoring the progression of each throughout, that it appears the brain must be doing many things at once.

Fortunately this switching can be trained, both by learning to use the brain's existing machinery more efficiently and by training your brain's basic task-switching ability.

To help with the first, I spoke with Claudia Roda, computer learning specialist at the American University of Paris. "I don't work on attention by chance. It's a product of myself," Roda told me, searching online for the name of a paper she'd written while we talked on the phone and she adjusted her chair and monitored e-mail. "But there are also things I can't do while talking on the phone," she says. "I can't actually read an e-mail or write a paper."

Roda says this illustrates a basic fact of multitasking (a word we'll continue to use as a shorthand): there are tasks we can combine and tasks we can't.

First, we have a general pool of attention that we can distribute as we see fit—the less attention a task draws from this pool, the better we can add it to the things we're already doing. You can walk and chew gum because neither requires much attention. That's not to say you can't learn to do two consuming tasks at once, only that you have to automate one, the other, or both until the sum of the attention required remains below your limit.

If you want to see what this trained-to-automaticity multitasking looks like, search YouTube for the words "Multitasking Pi." In the video a talented gentleman calling himself the Multitasking King recites the first one hundred digits of pi while standing one-footed on a balance board, dribbling a basketball with one hand, and bouncing a golf ball with a mallet in the other. It certainly looks like multitasking, but in fact the Multitasking King has trained each skill until it's not a task at all. Dribbling, balancing, bouncing, and reciting pi are all so automatic that together they sum to the equivalent of me walking and chewing gum.

The Multitasking King exploits another neat trick: the farther away tasks are in the brain, the easier they are to cobble together. For example, Broca's area of the brain is responsible for producing language and largely responsible for interpreting it, making it extremely difficult—as Roda points out—to talk on the phone and write an e-mail at the same time. But playing dodge ball lives in your primary motor cortex, way up in the middle-top of your brain, and so theoretically it should be perfectly possible to play dodge ball while talking on the phone if you were so inclined. The Multitasking King does something similar by pairing a demanding memory task with three very automatic gross motor tasks.

So to successfully combine tasks, imagine the four lobes of the brain: frontal, parietal, temporal, and occipital. To minimize interference between tasks, pick a task from each lobe rather than multiple tasks from the same—thinking, planning, and speech in the frontal lobe; spatial sense in the parietal; sound perception (but not speech processing!) in the temporal lobe; and visual processing in the occipital. Maybe you can even add balance or finely tuned movement from the cerebellum.

So now you have two strategies that will help you best use your existing task-switching abilities to approximate multitasking: automate tasks so they consume less attention and cherry-pick ones from distant areas of the brain.

As for the second, more practical piece of the multitasking puzzle—actually improving your brain's task-switching abilities— it's worth hopping right into practice. The first three exercises below train your ability to quickly apply simple sorting rules, each training a slightly different flavor of the skills needed for task switching. The fourth exercise combines these three simple rules into a fiendishly difficult task-switching challenge. And the fifth trains a slightly different variety of this skill.

EXERCISE 54
LETTER AND NUMBER SORT

This exercise is a stalwart of laboratory-based task-switching training programs. Copy, cut out, and arrange the following cards into a face-down deck. Now you'll sort them as quickly as possible into piles. Flip a card: if the lower symbol is a letter, sort the card according to whether the upper letter is a vowel or a consonant. If the upper letter is a vowel, put the card in a pile to your left. If it's a consonant, put it in a pile to your right. If the lower symbol is a number, sort the card according to whether the upper number is odd or even. If the upper number is odd, sort it to the left and if even, sort it to the right.

To complete this task successfully, your brain has to quickly flip back and forth between two rules—sorting by letter or by number— and if you keep practicing this exercise and improving your speed, your everyday task-switching ability will improve as well.

Here's another trick: once you understand these rules, ramp up the difficulty by swapping them. This time, if the bottom symbol is a letter, sort the card according to the upper number, etc. Or change the sorting *direction*—that is, put vowels and odd numbers to the right. With each pass through the deck, change the rules.

i4 e	S4 3	F3 P	Z7 2
U9 x	N6 4	e4 A	T5 7
J8 R	w1 5	F4 S	H3 6
A8 T	R7 8	B4 M	Y3 9

R3 e	B7 3	E8 P	Y6 2
V1 x	M9 4	c2 w	Q4 7
i9 R	P6 5	A4 S	G2 6
k5 T	L6 8	i5 w	o2 9

FRUIT AND VEGETABLE SORT

As in the previous exercise, the idea here is to copy, cut out, and arrange cards into a deck and sort them as quickly as you can. (Make two copies and then cut out the following fruit and vegetable cards.) Again, you'll alternate the rule you use to do the sorting. Sort the first card according to whether the food is drawn big or small. Then sort the next card according to fruit or vegetable. You'll end with four piles: fruit, vegetable, big, and small.

In fact this is a rare example of a non-IQ task that may bleed over into gains in intelligence. According to psychologist Julia Karbach, who has used this exercise extensively, that's because, "switching training imposes demands on other executive functions as well." In this exercise you not only practice task switching and must inhibit the previous rule but also depend on working memory to keep track of which rule

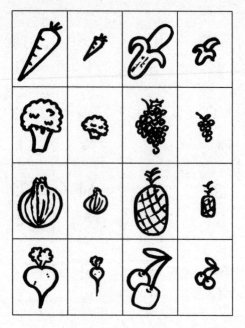

you're using. This trifecta makes for a powerful exercise, not only for multitasking but for fluid intelligence as well.

STROOP, THERE IT IS!

The Stroop effect describes the difficulty of recognizing the color *green* when the color is used to write the word *red*. The Stroop effect also rears its cognitively challenging head when using the term "bigger" to describe printed numbers. For instance, if you see the number 125 printed larger than the number 12,432, your brain is forced to struggle with the same kind of conflicting signals; numerically, one number is bigger; in terms of printed size, the other is.

As in the previous exercises, copy, cut, and stack the following cards into a facedown deck. Now flip two cards at a time. If both numbers are printed large or small, sort the cards according to which number is numerically bigger—the "bigger" card goes in a pile to the left;

the "smaller" card goes in a pile to the right. If one number is printed large and the other small, sort the cards according to which number is printed physically larger. While still heavy on task switching, the flavor of this exercise leans a little bit more toward impulse inhibition than the previous exercises. Admit it: it's hard to see the number 3 as larger than the number 8, even when it's printed as a Goliath to 8's David.

1	2	3	4
5	6	7	8
9	10	11	12
13	14	15	16

17	18	19	20
21	22	23	24
25	26	27	28
29	30	31	32

MULTITASKING CHALLENGE

Just as the Multitasking King described in this chapter's introduction practiced dribbling a basketball, reciting the digits of pi, and so on in order to automate tasks to the point he could perform them simultaneously, it's almost certainly necessary to practice this chapter's first three exercises before attempting to combine them in this one.

Shuffle the cards from the previous three exercises into one deck and review the exercises' sorting rules: by odd/even and consonant/vowel; by large/small and vegetable/fruit; and by printed large/small and numerically large/small. Now not only must you remember these complex sorting rules and inhibit the irrelevant ones, but you must remember back to previous cards to continue alternating each rule when appropriate (for example, did you sort the last food card according to size, or whether it was fruit or vegetable?).

Yep. This is really, really hard. But if you think about it, we place these kinds of demands on our brains every day—for instance, when you cook breakfast while getting dressed, remembering a shopping list, listening to the news, feeding pets, and checking e-mail (while swinging from a trapeze above a pool of sharks). Practice with this exercise will train your brain to navigate the demands of the real world.

TRAIL MAKER

Developed in 1944, the Trail Making Task is one of the most commonly used tests of task switching (although it also draws on visual search and processing speed). It's also a common component of tests for brain damage, used in hundreds of studies of brain lesions and the effects of potentially damaging experiences such as combat and abuse.

More important for our purposes, training with trail maker–like tasks has been shown to increase such things as the speed with which older adults can perform tasks of daily living and the decision-making speed of drivers.

This is basically a connect-the-dots exercise, without an obvious picture and with the twist that it makes you use symbols and rules to do the connecting, thus creating a challenge that forces your brain to monitor and switch between tasks. Use the instructions below to connect the dots in each picture.

1. Start with the number 1, then alternate letters and numbers in order (1, A, 2, B, 3, C, etc.)

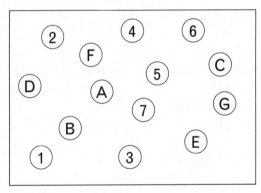

2. Alternate numbers, letters, and roman numerals in order (1, A, I, 2, B, II, etc.)

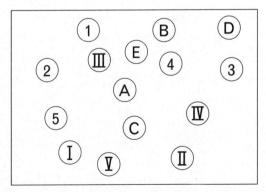

3. Alternate numbers with letters, but reverse the order of the numbers (7, A, 6, B, 5, C, etc.)

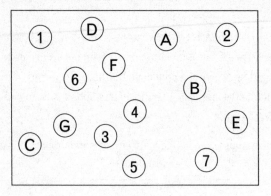

4. Alternate numbers with letters, but reverse the order of the letters (1, J, 2, I, 3, H, etc.)

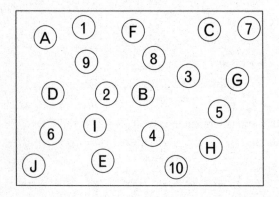

WIN AND FAIL MULTITASKING

Formula One driver Nelson Piquet famously called his onetime team-mate and most-of-the-time rival Nigel Mansell "an uneducated block-head with a stupid and ugly wife." And the two brought their beef to the 1987 British Grand Prix at the Silverstone Circuit, Mansell's home track. Within a handful of laps, Mansell's car developed a vibration in the front right tire and he had to pull into the pits. When he roared back twenty-nine seconds behind Piquet, Mansell told the Daily Mail, *"I was told on the pit board I was running out of fuel and I had to turn the engine down. So I had a lot of emotional things to deal with." Mansell had to inhibit the distractions of his waning fuel, the cheering crowd, the fears about his faulty car, and the hopelessness of being twenty-nine seconds back. He had to switch from noticing corner apexes to driving his line and monitoring his speed. And he had to do this while remembering the race positions and car conditions that affected strategy. When Mansell came across the line for the win, his fuel tank ran dry and he coasted to a stop. This is a multitasking win.*

A few years later, Mansell was leading the pack in the last lap of the 1991 Canadian Grand Prix, with rival Nelson Piquet a good couple of seconds back. And with the race seemingly in hand, Mansell tried to multitask by waving to the crowd. Only, he didn't smoothly switch tasks from driving, and while there's some debate over what exactly he did wrong—did he let his engine revs fall too low or accidentally flip the engine kill switch?—he somehow managed to stall in the last turn as Piquet zoomed elatedly past for the win. While Mansell later blamed the meltdown on a late gearbox failure, most think the gearbox that failed was the one in his head. This is a multitasking fail.

CHAPTER 15

HEURISTICS AND BIASES

A few months ago, a friend introduced me to the strategy game Carcassonne. I've been playing it compulsively in app form ever since. Basically, the game consists of picking and playing four-sided tiles on which are drawn bits of a medieval countryside—walled cities, roads, farms, and cloisters. Like dominoes, you have to match tiles in order to lay them down. For example, if a tile on the board shows a road exiting one side, you have to play a tile that continues the road. By using a limited number of tokens to claim these cities, farms, roads, and cloisters, you earn points.

And as I've been learning how to play, I've been wondering what are good and bad strategies. Should I immediately take any points I can get or invest my tiles to win more points later? Should I always try to claim the central farm or is it not worth worrying about farms until the final ten tiles? Should I only fight to steal a city from an opponent once the opponent has built it to a certain number of points? Should

I always have a city, a road, a cloister, and a farm in development so I can build my points with any type of tile?

In other words, I'm developing rules of thumb, deciding on the heuristics of best play. You live your life according to similar heuristics. These heuristics act as shortcuts—pressure-release valves that allow you to avoid the fate of the thousands of sci-fi robots from the 1960s through 1980s who fried their circuits while saying (robotically), "Does not compute! Does not compute! Does not compute!" and then exploding. When possible, we automate decisions and behaviors and so leave more brainpower for the few novel and challenging tasks we come across (see chapter 14 on multitasking). Like learning to play a game, you may design some of your own heuristics—for example, you might only cross streets if the Don't Walk hand has blinked fewer than four times. Or maybe you've decided to never date friends' exes.

You can also pick up heuristics from culture, for (tongue-in-cheek) example, the rule from the movie *The Princess Bride*: "Never go in against a Sicilian when death is on the line!" More seriously, Thomas Gilovich, behavioral economist at Cornell University, points to rules like "Buy the most expensive wine your budget allows," or "Play for a tie on the road or a win at home." Culture expresses many of its heuristics in the form of axioms like "Haste makes waste" and "Never look a gift horse in the mouth."

Finally you hold within you the layer of heuristics built by millions of years of evolution for the purpose of your continued aliveness. For example, in our caveman past, it wasn't worth taking a 50-50 stab at a mammoth. Instead, the only odds under which Thog was gonna poke a thirteen-foot-tall, nine-ton bulldozer might have been somewhere around 90/10 that said poking would result in food on the table and not just a pissed off bulldozer. Like many predators, Thog evolved risk aversion: the penalty for failure frequently outweighed the benefit of success. Evolution coded this risk aversion into our genome and thus our brains, and now in addition to convenient things like keeping us from trying to outrace closing train-crossing gates, it pops up in inconvenient places like bad bets on the stock market and in poker games. Would you bet $100 on a coin flip to win $210? If not, you're risk averse. Risk aversion leads to heuristics of caution like "Better safe than sorry" and "A bird in hand is worth two in the bush."

Risk aversion is certainly not alone among the heuristics gifted us by evolution. Take the anchoring heuristic, which makes us glue our opinions to certain facts while overlooking others. For example, a study in the *American Journal of Preventative Medicine* shows that homebuyers anchor their choice to a house's square footage while overlooking commute times. Unfortunately, the study also shows that in terms of happiness and well-being, commute times matter much more than the square footage of your house.

Or there's the famous availability heuristic, which explains why, after the kidnapping of Etan Patz in 1979, parents across the country kept their kids indoors. Did a kidnapper on the loose actually increase the chance that a child in Tallahassee or Des Moines would go missing? No. But Patz's picture on milk cartons put the possibility firmly front and center in parents' minds—it made the image available.

We're also biased to stick with our first opinions, recognizing only the "facts" that conform to what we already think. For example, Henning Plessner of the University of Heidelberg showed films of gymnastics competitions to a panel of trained judges. Traditionally, the best gymnasts are in the later rotations and, sure enough, judges' scores confirmed these expectations. But even when Plessner mixed the order of gymnasts to put better routines earlier, judges continued to give higher scores to the later, less skillful, performances. They had a theory that later gymnasts are better, and they stuck to it even in the face of contradictory evidence.

However, many of our heuristics are adaptive—helpful shortcuts that allow us to make good, quick decisions in the face of uncertainty. Without them, we'd be so lost in thought over every decision that we'd be unable to function. But as the above examples show, some of your personal heuristics may be plain wrong, and even some of the evolutionary heuristics could use an update.

Not only can revising heuristics make better rules, but Richard Crisp, psychologist at the University of Kent in the UK, says that as you practice overruling your rules of thumb you also train the overall cognitive flexibility needed to adapt to any challenging new experience.

Take racial and ethnic stereotyping, or what researchers call the representative heuristic (we imagine an individual's characteristics represent the perceived characteristics of their group). Crisp points out that, yes, we've evolved a powerful heuristic that allows us to quickly recognize, stereotype, and avoid people who are not like us— but we have a second system in place that can override this stereotype, evaluating a stranger from a strange group as a possible ally. We have a kneejerk response, but we also have cognitive control.

We naturally apply this layer of cognitive control when a heuristic fails. For example, Crisp shows that when subjects experience a person who breaks stereotype, such as a female mechanic, subjects sink into neither (for example) "female" nor "mechanic" stereotypes and instead more accurately evaluate the female mechanic based on other, individual information the researchers give them.

Here's the interesting part:

Overwriting a heuristic with analysis requires an awesome amount of cognitive control. So, "Long-term experience at multiculturalism actually improves people's cognitive flexibility," says Crisp. "If you consistently have to inhibit your stereotypes, ultimately the cognitive consequence of living in a diverse society is the release of heuristics in favor of the construction of new knowledge."

Living according to heuristics may be easy, but now that I can play

Carcassonne by rote rules, it's no fun anymore—I'm burned out, done with the game (and on to Kingdoms of Camelot). Life isn't nearly so simplistic and so there's no limit to the amount of new knowledge you can construct. That is, if you're willing to constantly question the rules by which you live your life.

|||||||||||||||||||||||||||||||||||||||| **EXERCISE 59** ||||||||||||||||||||||||||||||||||||||||
COUNTERFACTUAL THINKING

You miss the lottery by one number. You're the first car stuck behind an opening bridge. You miss a plane that crashes. These situations stimulate what researchers call counterfactual thinking—you can't help but imagine the near alternatives. In many ways, counterfactual thinking is the opposite of heuristics, in that heuristics provide a single, quick answer and counterfactual thinking provides a list of alternatives. And sure enough, psychologists show that asking the *what-ifs* of counterfactual thinking can help de-bias the kneejerk behaviors suggested by nearly any heuristic.

For example, researchers Adam Galinsky and Gordon Moskowitz had subjects imagine one of two scenarios. In the first, Sue is at a rock concert, switches seats, and then the person sitting in her old seat wins a prize. In the second scenario, Sue doesn't switch seats and some unrelated seat wins the prize. The first elicits counterfactual thinking in the form of agonizing over the decision to switch seats and imagining what might've been.

But here's the cool part: the subjects who were primed to think counterfactually were less likely to fall prey to the heuristic known as "confirmation bias" in an unrelated task—instead of finding evidence that confirmed the first theory they came up with, they appreciated the existence of many possible explanations and so evaluated new evidence without the cloud of preordained certainty. Further experiments by Galinsky confirmed that these counterfactual thinkers act rationally, as opposed to being led by the nose by heuristics and bias. Coincidentally (though not necessarily in the wheelhouse of bias and heuristic), Galinsky and his colleagues also found that counterfactual thinkers are consistently more motivated, which he explains as a heightened awareness that the present has meaning—there's more than one path pointing into the future, and your actions and decisions can define which path you go down.

Try it:

In the space below, list at least three turning points in your past, big or small, recent or long ago. Then list possible outcomes of different decisions, actions, or luck. How would your life be different? Now the real trick is not counterfactual thinking itself, which is relatively easy, but *remembering* to think counterfactually.

REALITY BIAS

The book *Dune* asks a simple question: What if we had no water? Of course, we *do* have water, at least for the time being, and so the book brazenly breaks a longstanding human bias—the reality bias. We are biased toward predictions and explanations that fit our implicitly understood experience of reality and tend not to consider possibilities outside what we see as this reality.

In the previous exercise, you worked to imagine plausible alternatives to plausible situations. In this exercise, you'll use similar counterfactual reasoning taken a step further to imagine plausible alternatives to *implausible* situations, thus learning to break this reality bias. Because the reality bias is a much-researched roadblock to creativity, this exercise could as easily have been included in chapter 4 on creativity.

List three consequences for each *Dune*-like statement of adjusted reality. See the Facebook page *Counterfactuals—Big Bang Theory* for more thought-provoking examples.

1. What would happen if snow were black?

2. What would happen if ice sank instead of floated?

3. What would happen if gravity worked in reverse and larger objects repelled instead of attracted?

4. What would happen if the shortest distance between two points were not a straight line?

5. What would happen if air were denser than water?

EXERCISE 61
HEURISTIC AWARENESS

This exercise will help you recognize common biases and heuristics so that you can choose to act on them or ignore them as appropriate instead of simply being led like a lemming off the cliff of illogic. We covered some of these heuristics in this chapter's introduction, but some are new. Answer the following questions to see if you fall prey to illogic, and then flip to the back to see what, if anything, led you astray.

1. Caroline and John are trying to decide between two brands of flat-screen televisions. *Consumer Reports* and general online

opinion tend to favor the Toshiko over the Mitsuhashi, but John *owned* a Toshiko and the thing fizzled after six months. How would you counsel this couple?

2. Which of the following two statements is logical? (1) No reptiles have fur; snakes are reptiles; therefore, snakes don't have fur. (2) All things with four legs are furry; hairless cats have four legs; therefore, hairless cats are furry.

3. Over a long career, Pete bats .314, meaning that he gets just over three hits per every ten at-bats. Then in one game, Pete gets three hits in his first three at-bats. What are his chances of getting a hit in his fourth at-bat? Are they greater, less than, or equal to .314?

4. The new wonder drug Pemexidran cures migraines but causes severe side effects in a small percentage of patients. Jacob has migraines and is considering Pemexidran, but his father-in-law who took the drug ended up in a wheelchair. How would you counsel Jacob?

5. The leading batting average a month into any baseball season is usually around .450, but no one ever ends with .450. Why not?

6. There are thirty-one balls in a bucket. Ten are red and the remaining balls are split between white and black. If you name the color and then draw it blind, you win $100. What color should you name?

7. When you combine measurements from the Great Pyramid of Giza, you can get 6/9/2009—the date of Michael Jackson's death. Is that freaky or what?

8. Do you think the population of Botswana is greater or less than forty million? Without looking online, what's your best guess at this country's population?

9. Here's an abbreviation of a famous problem by Amos Tversky and Daniel Kahneman: Linda is thirty-one years old, single, outspoken, and smart. She's concerned with issues of social justice and discrimination. Is it more likely Linda is a bank teller, or that she is a bank teller and an active feminist?

10. Psychologists found that 93 percent of PhD candidates registered early when threatened with a penalty for late registration, whereas only 67 percent registered early when the choice was presented as a discount for early registration. Why do you think that might be?

11. In the O.J. Simpson murder trial, Johnnie Cochran repeatedly said of the famous glove, "If it doesn't fit, you must acquit." How do you rate this reasoning?

<hr />

EXERCISE 62

BIASES, HEURISTICS, AND LOGICAL FALLACIES

OK, I admit we've played fast and loose with the terms *heuristic* and *bias*. According to people who care about these semantics, heuristics can create cognitive biases—and modern psychologists have added to the list of these biases many of the things the Greeks called logical *fallacies*. Sure, sure—there are some fallacies that shouldn't be included on the bias list and vice versa (and heuristics are another thing altogether), but there's certainly enough overlap to justify a look at fallacies in this chapter. And as in the previous exercise, by learning to recognize these fallacies in their natural settings, you can learn to avoid them when appropriate.

Preview the following logical fallacies and then match them with the given examples from media. Granted, even in short quotations some of the following people are able to pack in more than one fallacy, so when ambiguity exists, pick the best fallacy from many correct possibilities.

LOGICAL FALLACIES

- Improper transposition: knowing only that one thing follows another implies nothing about what happens when the first thing is absent.

- False dilemma: two alternatives are presented as the only options, when other alternatives exist.

- Appeal to nature: what is natural is good.

- Denying the antecedent: the common fallacy in the form if A, then B. Not A, so not B.

- Scope fallacy: ambiguity in whether a modifier applies to what comes before or after. For example, *all that glitters is not gold.* What the heck kind of metal is "not gold"?

- Ambiguity: linguistic ambiguity makes a statement seem valid when in fact it's incorrect or at least misleading.

- Guilt by association: nothing good can possibly be associated with something bad.

- Appeal to authority: it's true because an expert says it's true.

- *Tu quoque* (You also): turning the accusation back on the accuser.

- *Post hoc ergo propter hoc*: correlation doesn't necessarily imply causation.

FALLACIES IN THE MEDIA

1. Benjamin Disraeli, when ordered to withdraw his declaration that half the Cabinet were asses: "Mr. Speaker, I withdraw. Half the Cabinet are not asses."

Source: Sarah Lyall, "The Right Hon. Twerp Debates the Windbag," *New York Times,* February 26, 1995

2. "I did not have sexual relations with that woman, Miss Lewinsky."

Source: Bill Clinton, White House news conference on education, January 26, 1998

3. Tom Cruise disparaging psychiatry as a Nazi science: "Well, look at the history. Jung was an editor for the Nazi papers during World War II . . . . Look at the experimentation the Nazis did with electric shock and drugging. Look at the drug methadone. That was originally called Adolophine. It was named after Adolf Hitler."

Source: "Q&A: Tom Cruise," *Entertainment Weekly,* June 9, 2005

4. "TASTE NATURE. AND NOTHING ELSE. You'll never find any additives in our tobacco. What you see is what you get. Simply 100% whole-leaf natural tobacco. True authentic tobacco taste. It's only natural."

Source: Ad for American Spirit cigarettes, *Discover Magazine,* May 2007

5. Alan Turing intentionally flubbing logic: "If each man had a definite set of rules of conduct by which he regulated his life he would be no better than a machine. But there are no such rules, so men cannot be machines."

Source: Alan Turing, *Computing Machinery and Intelligence,* 1950

6. Osama bin Laden responding to accusation of funding terrorism: "At the same time that they condemn any Muslim who calls for his rights, they receive the top official of the Irish Republican Army at the White House as a political leader."

Source: Kate Zernike, "The Death of Osama Bin Laden," *New York Times,* May 2, 2011

7. Tim Pawlenty, in support of his plan to overhaul Medicare: "If it was a choice between [my plan and] Barack Obama's plan of doing nothing?"

Source: E. Magill, "5 Fallacies from the Republican Debate," *Salon,* June 15, 2011

8. Michele Bachmann: "The CBO, the Congressional Budget Office, has said that Obamacare will kill 800,000 jobs. What could the president be thinking by passing a bill like this, knowing full well it will kill 800,000 jobs?"

Source: E. Magill, "5 Fallacies from the Republican Debate," *Salon,* June 15, 2011

9. "The idea that vaccines are a primary cause of autism is not as crackpot as some might wish. Autism's 60-fold rise in 30 years matches a tripling of the U.S. vaccine schedule."

Source: Jenny McCarthy, "Who's Afraid of the Truth About Autism?" *Huffington Post,* March 9, 2010

10. President George W. Bush: "You're either with us or against us in the fight against terror."

Source: CNN.com, November 6, 2001

THE AFFECT HEURISTIC AND MORAL ALGEBRA

To Charles Darwin, the question of marriage felt ruled by emotion—psychologists would say he felt led by the "affect heuristic." To de-bias his thinking, Darwin used a moral algebra developed by Benjamin Franklin to weigh the pluses and minuses of marriage. In the "Marry" column, Darwin's entries include, "Children (if it please God), object to be beloved & played with, better than a dog anyhow, charms of music and female chit-chat, picture to yourself a nice soft wife on a sofa with a good fire." And in the "Not Marry" column he wrote, "Conversation of clever men at clubs, not forced to visit relatives & bend to every trifle, fatness & idleness, less money for books." Below the chart, he scrawled, "Then how should I manage all my business if I were obliged to go every day walking with my wife—Eheu!!" The next year, he married Emma Wedgwood and the couple had ten children. De-biased, indeed!

1. REMOTE ASSOCIATION

fire/ranger/tropical = *forest*

carpet/alert/herring = *red*

forest/fly/fighter = *fire*

cane/daddy/plum = *sugar*

friend/flower/scout = *girl*

duct/worm/video = *tape*

sense/room/place = *common*

pope/eggs/Arnold = *Benedict*

fair/mind/dating = *game*

date/duck/fold = *blind*

cadet/outer/ship = *space*

dew/badger/bee = *honey*

ash/luck/belly = *pot*

break/food/forward = *fast*

nuclear/feud/values = *family*

collector/duck/fold = *bill*

car/French/shoe = *horn*

office/mail/step = *box*

circus/around/car = *clown*

sand/age/mile = *stone*

catcher/dirty/hot = *dog*

fly/milk/peanut = *butter*

tank/notch/secret = *top*

thief/cash/larceny = *petty*

artist/great/route = *escape*

hammer/line/hunter = *head*

blank/gut/mate = *check*

list/circuit/cake = *short*

master/child/piano = *grand*

cover/line/wear = *under*

beer/pot/laugh = *belly*

trip/left/goal = *field*

blue/light/rocket = *sky*

man/sonic/star = *super*

bus/illness/computer = *terminal*

type/ghost/sky = *writer*

full/punk/engine = *steam*

break/black/cake = *coffee*

car/human/drag = *race*

liberty/bottom/curve = *bell*

drunk/line/fruit = *punch*

buster/bird/wash = *brain*

fruit/hour/napkin = *cocktail*

old/dog/joke = *fart*

toad/sample/foot = *stool*

2. FUNCTIONAL FIXEDNESS

1. Remember the Duncker candle problem? In this case, like the box of tacks, a holder is more than a holder. Remove the sleeping bag from its sack and then slip the sack over the forked branch to make a paddle.

2. Did you disassemble the pen in your mind to discover a hollow plastic tube? If so, you might have guessed that MacGyver cuts the fuel line and rejoins it so that fuel flows through the hollow pen tube.

3. The reason you likely got this one quickly is that you didn't have to stray far from your functional fixedness of a gutter's common use. Instead of transporting rainwater, MacGyver uses the gutter to transport diamonds. The lampshade is a funnel.

4. Renaming the "scarf" as a *length of cloth* may have helped you see that it could be used as a sling with the rock as its projectile. Now unseating a bad guy just takes good aim.

5. Dutch lensmaker Hans Lippershey invented the first telescope in 1608. MacGyver's answer to this puzzle is a twist on the classic, with newspaper rolled into a tube and the watch crystal opposite the magnifying glass at the open ends.

6. MacGyver fills the plastic bags with water and ties them to either side of a length of fishing line. He wraps the line around the knob so that water bags hang off either side, then pokes a hole in one bag. As that bag lightens, the other drops and the knob turns.

7. He pours the water into the radiator and starts the car. When the water heats up, he cracks the eggs into the radiator. As they cook, the egg whites plug the slow leaks.

8. The rake head is a grappling hook and the garden hose is rope. As you progress through these puzzles, are you finding it easier to release functional fixedness?

9. The soccer ball is a red herring, used only as a mold to sculpt the newspaper into the shape of a spherical hot-air balloon, which is powered by flaming cotton balls.

10. A bicycle is made of many parts, and so if you deconstructed it in your mind, you can probably imagine a couple of ways to shoot a ball bearing. MacGyver's answer was to make a slingshot from the handlebars and an inner tube.

3. REBUS ROUNDUP

1. Dark ages
2. Big bad wolf
3. Capital punishment
4. Little league
5. Grave error
6. Ambiguous
7. Excuse me
8. Tea for two
9. Go stand in the corner
10. A round of applause
11. Split personality
12. Waterfall (or standing water)
13. Paralegal
14. Too big to ignore
15. Sit down and shut up
16. Search high and low
17. Somewhere over the rainbow
18. A home away from home
19. Beating around the bush
20. Diamond in the rough
21. A little on the large side
22. Just between friends
23. Lying down on the job
24. Rock around the clock

4. INSIGHT FINAL EXAM

Congratulations to anyone who got "broad jump" or "money belt"!

board/blade/back = *switch*

land/hand/house = *farm*

hungry/order/belt = *money*

forward/flush/razor = *straight*

shadow/chart/drop = *eye*

way/ground/weather = *fair*

cast/side/jump = *broad*

back/step/screen = *door*

reading/service/stick = *lip*

over/plant/horse = *power*

5. WASON SELECTION TASK: EVIDENCE FOR PRACTICAL INTELLIGENCE

In general, the Wason Selection Task requires realizing that in each case, you only have to find a condition that would falsify the claim—not conditions that would lend it further support. Only about 10 percent of people get the first two questions right. But about 75 percent get the third and fourth questions right. To Leda Cosmides, John Tooby, and other evolutionary psychologists, this is because we have evolved the ability to reason about the real world much more accurately than we reason about abstract problems. In other words, evolution has hardwired us for a practical intelligence that is distinct from general intelligence.

Here, finally, are the answers:

1. If there were a square on the back of the 4, or an even number on the back of the square, it would negate the claim. Did you flip the star too? There's no need. No matter if the number on back is even or odd, it would do nothing to negate the claim that even numbers hold stars.

2. Same here—did you flip the 4? You don't have to. Only finding an odd number on the A or a vowel on the 7 would negate the claim.

3. In this classic case, it's easier to see that you have to test that the seventeen-year-old isn't drinking alcohol, and test that the beer isn't being consumed by anyone under twenty-one. It doesn't matter what the twenty-three-year-old is drinking and it doesn't matter who's having the soda.

4. Finally, you have to make sure that the thing that went up came down, and that the thing that never came down didn't ever go up in the first place. Flip "went up" and "didn't come down" to check.

6. IF, THEN, BECAUSE: MAKE IMPLICIT LEARNING EXPLICIT

N/A

7. SITUATIONAL JUDGMENT TEST

Generally, situational judgment tests (SJTs) are scored by measuring participants' responses against the responses of top performers—for example, comparing a job candidate's answers to the answers chosen by a panel of the best employees. In this case, the scenarios and best answers are adapted from ones used in a number of existing SJTs, though the situations involved are also very social and so the specifics of your job or your neighbor might affect the "best" actions.

1. *Best:* (B) Quietly decline the request. *Worst:* (A) Quietly accept the friend request.

2. *Best:* (C) Wait for twenty minutes and then talk to your friend about the appropriateness of her actions. *Worst:* (B) Placate watching parents by immediately explaining to your friend that disagreement between kids is normal and offer to teach your friend mediation techniques.

3. *Best:* (C) Explain to your crew that your head's on the line and you really need their help to make the deadline. *Worst:* (D) Do nothing. Delays in roadwork happen all the time and being behind schedule in this case is perfectly understandable.

4. *Best:* (D) Bring your neighbor a six-pack of Pabst Blue Ribbon as a thank-you for letting you borrow the mower. Wait until he's had at least two before explaining what happened. *Worst:* (B) Bring your neighbor to the scorched circle and insist he pay for nine square feet of sod to cover the hole.

5. *Best:* (B) Do nothing and hope that your job performance eventually speaks for itself. *Worst:* (A) Ask for a demotion so that you can work your way up from the bottom like everyone else.

6. *Best:* (C) Laugh and suggest that everyone must have strange mannerisms, and as an example offer a lighthearted impression of your unkind coworker. *Worst:* (A) Stop the meeting and ask to be assigned to a different group.

7. *Best:* (D) Have a private heart-to-heart with your coworker, explaining your concerns. *Worst:* (C) Next Monday, buy a plate of treats from the best bakery in town and anonymously set it next to your coworker's underpowered treats in the lunchroom. See what happens.

8. *Best:* (C) Don't touch it with a ten-foot pole. You want no part in this mother's eventual realization. *Worst:* (B) Suggest that perhaps cooing about her beautiful baby in public may make parents with less beautiful children feel bad.

9. *Best (though this is by far the most ambiguous—don't you think?):* (D) Be friendly and engage the mother in chitchat. Then suggest support services in the community for struggling parents. *Worst:* (B) Pointedly

suggest that if the wine seems a less good deal without the coupon, per-haps the mother might opt for the milk and corn, instead.

8. NONSENSE AND IMPLICIT LEARNING
N/A

9. IMPLICIT LEARNING TEST

In this test, there are 12 prototypical dingbits (P)—beetles that share all nine dingbit features. There are also 24 low-distortion dingbits with one or two changed features (LD); 24 neutral non-dingbits with three to six distor-tions (N); 24 high-distortion non-dingbits with seven or eight changed fea-tures (HD); and 12 anti-dingbits that share none of the prototypical dingbit features (A). Compare the solutions to your answers. Now add up the incor-rect answers for each of the types, P, LD, N, HD, and A. What percentage of each type did you label as a dingbit? Was it 100 percent of P's and 0 percent of A's? If you chose to complete half the test, then train implicit learning, and return for the second half, did your percentages change?

In Knowlton and Squire's experiment (in which they used giraffe-like animals and the category "peggle"), both amnesiacs and healthy subjects correctly called about 90 percent of the prototypical animals peggles, 80 percent of the low-distortion animals peggles, about 60 percent of the neutral animals peggles (oops!), about 40 percent of the high-distortion animals peggles (double oops!), and incorrectly labeled about 25 percent of the anti-peggles as peggles (triple oops!). How does your implicit cat-egory learning stack up?

N	LD	A	HD	N	LD
HD	N	HD	N	P	HD
HD	P	LD	A	HD	LD
LD	N	P	N	LD	HD
P	HD	LD	A	LD	HD
LD	A	N	P	N	LD
N	P	LD	HD	A	HD
A	N	N	LD	HD	N

N	HD	P	HD	LD	N
HD	LD	HD	LD	A	HD
LD	A	N	P	HD	N
HD	LD	LD	N	A	LD
P	N	A	N	P	HD
LD	A	LD	P	LD	N
HD	P	N	N	N	HD
LD	HD	LD	N	A	HD

10. PROBLEM-SOLVING OPERATIONS: RANDOM, DEPTH-FIRST, BREADTH-FIRST, AND MEANS-ENDS ANALYSIS SEARCH

N/A

11. MATCH: INITIAL STATE TO OPERATIONS

1. Depth-first search: There's a specific order in which these things must be done, for example underwear before pants. Once you've made an underwear choice, it's counterproductive to revisit the decision. Depth-first allows one pass through the system, generating one solution.

2. Breadth-first search: This is a thinly disguised maze problem—a depth-first search generates many solutions, which you can then compare.

3. Random search: It's quicker and easier to pick socks than it is to wonder what is the best strategy for picking socks.

4. Means-ends analysis: To close the gap between your current state (hungry) and your goal state (not hungry) requires the subgoal of moving away from the vending machine, to the ATM, before returning with cash.

12. FALSE ASSUMPTIONS

1. Feisty Kindergarteners

Assumption: All the kindergarteners must be on the ground. It's impossible to arrange four points equidistantly from each other on a plane. But stick one of the kindergarteners on the play structure and the other three in an equilateral triangle at its base and it's easy.

2. Battleship

Assumption: The lines must be horizontal or vertical columns or rows of evenly spaced stars. Also, if you thought of a star, this seductive but incorrect answer could have formed its own false assumption.

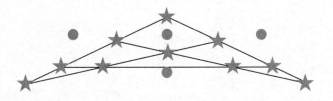

3. Car Trouble

Assumption: You must be the driver. Instead, give the keys to your best friend, who takes the old lady to the hospital while you wait for the bus with your dream date (who is now duly impressed).

4. Household Pets

Assumption: All households have *some* pets. Instead, all it takes is one petless household for the product of all pets in US households to be exactly zero.

5. Coconut Grove

Assumption: The doors opened outward. Instead, the doors of the Coconut Grove nightclub opened inward, and with people pressed against them, they couldn't be opened. In modern buildings, doors open out.

6. *Not* That *Prisoner's Dilemma*

Assumption: The prisoner cut the rope in half along its width. Instead, the prisoner divides the rope in half *lengthwise*. When he ties these two strands together, the rope is twice its original length. (Apparently it's still strong enough to hold him.)

7. Cut the Card

Assumption: The edges of the card must maintain their original dimensions. Instead:

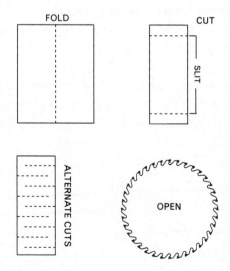

8. Socks in a Drawer

Assumption: The ratio 5:4 matters. Without this assumption, you see that at the unluckiest, you will draw one white sock and one black sock, at which point the third sock you draw is guaranteed to match one already drawn, giving you a pair. The maximum number of socks you must draw to guarantee a pair is 3.

9. Jane and Janet

Assumption: Jane and Janet are the only siblings born. In fact, they are triplets (or quads, or quints, etc.) with an unmentioned child or children and thus not twins. Another answer is to imagine Jane and Janet as children of a lesbian couple with simultaneous due dates, making them sisters by family but not by blood.

10. Matchstick Math

Assumption: You can only move matchsticks that make roman numerals. Instead, move a stick that makes one of the operators, as follows:

13. SLIDING TILE PUZZLES

N/A

14. INSPIRED, DIVERGENT THINKING

N/A

15. THE BOOK OF NONSENSE

N/A

16. FIGURE COMPLETION

N/A

17. EMBODIED COGNITION

N/A

18. CREATIVITY GRAB BAG
N/A

19. RUBE GOLDBERG MACHINE DESIGN CHALLENGE
N/A

20. RETRAIN ATTENTION, RETRAIN INTUITION
N/A

21. KIND AND WICKED INTUITION

1. Without follow-up from the specialist, feedback is nonexistent. Your intuition may be comparing this case to similar, previous cases, but without knowing how any of these cases resolve, this wicked training environment can lead to incorrect intuition.

2. A strange shirt in the laundry was unambiguous feedback. But it was only one case. Beware what Eugene Sadler-Smith calls the tyranny of small numbers.

3. Similar to the ER doc in the first example, an HR manager who never hears about job performance trains intuition in a wicked environment. Sure, your intuition separates the wheat from the chaff, but then, without feedback, how can you know if your guess was right or wrong?

4. Mightn't candidates' job success be due to six months of training rather than to your evaluation of their skills? Like this chapter's example of the waitress who intuits that well-dressed people tip more, and then creates evidence for it by treating these customers better, perhaps training creates the connection between candidates and success.

5. With consistent, relevant, unambiguous feedback, this is a kind training environment.

6. Certainly this is a wicked training environment—feedback is ambiguous and perhaps your coworker's terseness has nothing to do with you at all. However, human intuition about others' emotions is notoriously precise. In situations of social intuition, ask yourself how much information you may be taking in subconsciously. Does this extra information still

leave you stranded in a wicked training environment, or are things perhaps kinder than you initially thought?

22. ARTIFICIAL GRAMMAR

About that rule: following is a diagram of the artificial grammar used to create the letter strings in this exercise.

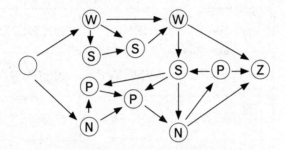

Starting at the first, empty dot and following the arrows, the rule takes only permissible paths through the chart. So you could take the path WSSWZ, but can never get the letter pairs WN, WP, SZ, PW, NW, and NS. Letter strings that contain these pairings are illegal. And in the test portion of this exercise, legal strings were intermixed with strings that were identical but for the insertion of one of these illegal pairings. The answers follow.

How did you do? In a study that compared the performance of healthy and amnesiac subjects on this artificial grammar task, psychologists Barbara Knowlton and Larry Squire found that healthy subjects correctly identified 63.5 percent of the grammatical items while incorrectly thinking that 41.5 percent of the non-grammatical items also fit the rule. Amnesiacs performed almost identically, further showing that intuitive learning is independent of traditional learning. These results mean that on this test, you should've correctly circled about ten of the grammatical items along with six of the non-grammatical items. If you beat the mean, give yourself a pat on the back for being especially intuitive. If not, consider searching online for further examples of artificial grammar tasks to train this skill.

23. DIY TDCS

N/A

24. DELIBERATE PRACTICE

N/A

25. DELIBERATE PERFORMANCE

N/A

26. EXPERT MEMORY

N/A

27. DIGIT SPAN

N/A

28. N-BACK

N/A

29. SIMON SAYS

N/A

30. ACTIVE

Pretest Answers

1-c, 2-j, 3-a, 4-e, 5-g, 6-t, 7-m, 8-n, 9-v, 10-p, 11-t, 12-r, 13-t, 14-e, 15-i

Letter Series Training

The first task of training is a scaled-down version of the test. Here, in each set of four letter pairs, circle the pair that doesn't belong.

1. AB, TS, XY, GH	9. BC, LM, PR, HI
2. GJ, NQ, KM, DG	10. Jj, Ii, kK, Hh
3. UV, PO, ML, DC	11. CH, HM, FK, NR
4. BB, BB, BC, BB	12. EC, BA, NL, HF
5. JK, HG, EF, NO	13. IJ, CD, LM, PO
6. JI, ON, BD, GF	14. DF, GF, VU, JI
7. Dd, FF, pP, JK	15. FH, PR, DE, TV
8. IK, BD, PS, LN	16. ON, FE, HI, KJ

You may have noticed certain kinds of relationships in these letter pairs. In the series themselves, these relationships are frequently hidden inside longer strings. And so the ACTIVE training taught participants to recognize the following four kinds of patterns:

- Identity: A pattern in which a chunk, however long, is cycled or periodically repeats without change—for example, trkodtrkodtrko ... or the *n*'s in annbnncnndnnenn ...
- Next: Sequential patterns, in most cases with chunks following alphabetical order—for example, abstcduvefwx ...
- Skip: Similar to "next" but with predictable holes in the sequence—for example, acegikmo ...
- Backward: Instances of the first three series, reversed—for example, gfedcbazy ...

The training also taught participants how to diagram letter series to represent these patterns. When you see repeating snippets ("identity"), underline them. Use brackets to show any instances of alphabetical order, as in "next." Make tick marks to show letters skipped in a pattern. Mark slashes in the string to show repetitions or "periods" in the pattern. Mark a left-pointing arrow above letters to show "backward." Here are examples from the pretest, diagrammed to show patterns:

1. [b   c]/[b   c]/[b   c]/[b   c]/b ...
2. f f [f   g] g [g   h] h [h   i] i [i   j] ...
3. g f e/f e d/e d c/d c b ...
4. [t   u][b   c][u   v][c   d][v   w]d ...
5. c ' e x/d ' f x/e ' g x/f ' h x/ ...
6. [h   i] p/[i   j] q/[j   k] r/[k   l] s/[l   m] ...

Now it's your turn to practice diagramming the patterns in letter series. Underline and draw brackets, tick marks, and slashes to show the patterns in the remaining items from the pretest:

7. e f b g h b i j b k l b ...

8. h i j k i j k l j k l m k l m ...

9. t p q t q r t r s t s t t t u t u ...

10. p m o p n o p o o p p o ...

11. x b q x c r x d s x e ...

12. a b v a b u a b t a b s a b ...

13. t o n t a t t o n t a ...
14. e m o e r o e n o e q o e o o ...
15. e f t u f g u v g h v w h ...

Test Answers

1-b, 2-f, 3-e, 4-u, 5-x, 6-t, 7-k, 8-v, 9-t, 10-f, 11-m, 12-p, 13-i, 14-g, 15-o.

Did you improve? In fact, these are the same patterns as in the pretest, only starting in difference places. Here is how the questions were reordered in the test: 13-1, 3-2, 6-3, 14-4, 7-5, 1-6, 15-7, 8-8, 9-9,10-10, 5-11, 2-12, 11-13, 4-14, 12-15. Are there patterns you missed both times? If so, take another look at how you diagrammed these series in the test. Now write out these twice-missed patterns yourself, starting at a different letter of the alphabet. Don't forget to search online for additional opportunities to practice your new pattern-recognition skills.

31. A COGNITIVELY INVOLVED LIFESTYLE

N/A

32. A COGNITIVELY KIND LIFESTYLE

N/A

33. THE WISDOM OF PROVERBS

Paul Baltes showed three life tasks that are especially necessary for the development of wisdom: selection, optimization, and compensation (SOC). Basically, in selection we set goals, in optimization we choose a strategy to pursue them, and then in compensation we reflect on outcomes that may not be quite what we intended. To Baltes, this SOC framework allows a person to tenaciously pursue goals but also gives them the vision to adapt them when necessary. And by passing many times through the selection-optimization-compensation cycle, we train wisdom.

According to Baltes's extensive testing and validation, the proverbs in this test are or aren't representative of SOC values. For example, *When the wind doesn't blow, grab the oars* represents compensation, the "C" in SOC. These SOC proverbs, he writes, "reflect active life-management strategies such as developing clear goals, investing into goal pursuit, and maintenance in the face of losses." Unfortunately, other proverbs like *Good things come to those who wait* represent the non-SOC values of "a relaxed life style, waiting for opportunities and good fortune to present itself, and giving in to losses," Baltes says.

Score your proverb choices according to the following answers. More than twelve correct implies wisdom. Then reflect on your incorrect answers. Why was the other answer wiser? In what way does it more accurately match Baltes's SOC framework? Baltes shows that this reflection leads to wisdom.

1. A—Optimization
2. A—Selection
3. B—Compensation
4. A—Selection
5. B—Selection
6. B—Compensation
7. B—Optimization
8. A—Optimization
9. A—Compensation
10. B—Optimization
11. B—Selection
12. A—Optimization
13. B—Optimization
14. A—Selection
15. A—Compensation
16. B—Selection
17. B—Compensation
18. A—Compensation

34. IMAGINE WISDOM

N/A

35. MORAL REASONING

Harvard and University of Chicago psychologist Lawrence Kohlberg pioneered the idea of stages of moral development—basically, the goal of this exercise is to help you progress through them. First mine your written answers for reasoning that aligns with Kohlberg's stages, listed below from lowest to highest—what's your baseline level of moral reasoning? Then revise your answers to address concerns from higher on the scale of moral reasoning. Here, in condensed form, are descriptions of Kohlberg's stages:

1. *Obedience and punishment:* Others are nonexistent and right and wrong depend on immediate reward and punishment.

2. *Self-interest:* Others exist but only insofar as they can further the

reasoner's self-interest—right and wrong depend on what you can gain from a choice.

3. *Conformity:* The reasoner wants to be liked and approved of by others and by society—choices depend on conforming to understood norms.

4. *Law-and-order:* Right and wrong exist to maintain social order and for that reason laws must be obeyed. If one person disobeyed the law, maybe many would.

5. *Human rights:* Right and wrong are calculated based on respect for basic rights like life and justice, and when laws violate rights, rights take precedence.

6. *Universal human ethics:* Reasoning takes into account multiple individual viewpoints and right and wrong are calculated selflessly based on the sum of benefit.

36. TEACH TO THE TESTS

N/A

37. ANCIENT WISDOM VS. NONSENSE

Nonsense:
The gleaming darkness confounds the fault.

Ancient Wisdom:
Swift as the wind, quiet as the forest, conquer like the fire, steady as the mountain—*The Art of War*

Some divisibility reveals the passion of any original void.

Pretend inferiority and encourage his arrogance—*The Art of War*

Any universal thought destroys the spirit, which is the brilliant totality.

When torrential water tosses boulders, it is because of its momentum—*The Art of War*

A dream presupposes wisdom: it is the immanent decision.

I know the joy of fishes in the river through my own joy, as I go walking along the same river—Chuang-Tzu

Nonsense:

The baster makes a good chicken nervous.

High-five is a skin ballot.

Any fertile vision is balanced by passion.

Any light cannot be the charm of our omnipotent passage.

Ignorance is enhanced by the prudence of the benevolent thought.

A thesis presupposes the waste of this gleaming sky.

The pure thought falsifies any passion.

Should a bass frown at an insult?

Ancient Wisdom:

Where can I find a man who has forgotten words so I can have a word with him?—Chuang-Tzu

A frog in a well cannot conceive of the ocean—Chuang-Tzu

This thaw took a while to thaw, it's going to take a while to unthaw—George W. Bush

One of the things important about history is to remember the true history—George W. Bush

Our thinking and our behavior are always in anticipation of a response—Deepak Chopra

One moon shows in every pool, in every pool the one moon—Zen saying

In theory there is no difference between theory and practice. In practice there is—Yogi Berra

A man who carries a cat by the tail learns something he can learn in no other way—Mark Twain

Nonsense:

A wheel clicks before a sniff.

Ancient Wisdom:

All you need is ignorance and confidence and then success is sure—Mark Twain

The poet extends into the rabbit.

Civilization is the limitless multiplication of unnecessary necessities—Mark Twain

The idea of the hidden performs the epistemology of unsituated knowledge.

The physical world, including our bodies, is a response of the observer—Deepak Chopra

38. INTRINSIC VS. EXTRINSIC MOTIVATION

N/A

39. COGNITIVE INTERVIEW

N/A

40. COMBATTING EXPERT CHOKING

N/A

41. COMBATTING NOVICE CHOKING

N/A

42. PRACTICE LIKE YOU PLAY (SO YOU CAN PLAY LIKE YOU PRACTICE)

N/A

43. RECOGNIZING AND LABELING EMOTIONS

N/A

44. UNDERSTANDING EMOTIONS

N/A

45. EXPRESSING EMOTIONS
N/A

46. REGULATING EMOTION
N/A

47. WORDS AND MEANING
N/A

48. NEURAL REPROCESSING
N/A

49. GRAMMATICAL REASONING
N/A

50. PAIRED ASSOCIATES
N/A

51. COUNT TO TEN
N/A

52. AVOID TEMPTATION (SO YOU DON'T HAVE TO RESIST IT)
N/A

53. THE WELL OF WILLPOWER
N/A

54. LETTER AND NUMBER SORT
N/A

55. FRUIT AND VEGETABLE SORT
N/A

56. STROOP, THERE IT IS!
N/A

57. MULTITASKING CHALLENGE

N/A

58. TRAIL MAKER

N/A

59. COUNTERFACTUAL THINKING

N/A

60. REALITY BIAS

N/A

61. HEURISTIC AWARENESS

1. Despite a much larger sample screaming otherwise, to Caroline and John the image of John's fizzled TV is immediately *available*. This is the availability heuristic—we're prone to making decisions based on first images, information, or memories that pop to mind, not necessarily the overall most *likely* images, information, or memories.

2. In the way this information is presented, both statements are logical. This, despite the *belief bias* screaming that hairless cats can't be furry. Did you disregard logic in favor of what you generally hold to be true?

3. This is the *gambler's fallacy* (or some people go even further to call it the *hot hand fallacy*): every time Pete steps to the plate he has an independent .314 chance of getting a hit, despite three lucky at-bats in a row. It's like a coin flip: every time you flip a coin the odds are 50-50 no matter how many heads you've previously flipped in a row. Despite the streak, Pete has the same chance he's always had of getting a hit (unless his three hits in a row slightly raised his batting average).

4. Jacob shouldn't let his father-in-law's experience stop him from taking the drug; it doesn't have any effect on his likelihood of having the same response to it. Our oversized tendency to respond to this kind of individual anecdote could be called the availability heuristic at work again, but psychologists also call this a *base rate fallacy*: we're likely to base our opinions on one personal case rather than the statistics of the larger system.

5. This is a classic example of *small sample bias* butting heads with the statistical phenomenon known as *regression to the mean.* Early in a baseball season, players have only a few at-bats—a "small sample" of what they'll have by the end of the season. You might hit a lucky .450 over the season's first twenty at-bats, but come October and 550-ish at-bats later, players tend to regress to the mean, sinking into more realistic batting averages.

6. Most people choose the only color they shouldn't: red. This is due to the *ambiguity bias*—you don't know if there are 2 or 21 white or black balls and so red seems like the surest bet. That's despite probability putting 10.5 white or black balls in the bag compared to only 10 red ones.

7. There are many possible measurements of the Great Pyramid, which can be combined in myriad ways, including—yes—to get the date of Michael Jackson's death, or pretty much anything else if you put your mind to it. This is *confirmation bias*—cherry-picking only the information that supports our preconceived point of view.

8. In fact, the population of Botswana is about two million. But your guess was likely much higher due to the *anchoring bias.* Like Steve Jobs pricing the iPhone at $500, anchoring the possible population of Botswana at forty million made it seem not only possible but likely.

9. Did you join 90 percent of Tversky and Kahneman's subjects in thinking it more likely Linda is both bank teller and feminist? If you stop to think about it for a minute, you realize that in order for that to be true, the first statement (that she's just a bank teller) must also be true. This is the *conjunction fallacy*—we assume specific things that make intuitive sense are more likely than a less well-supported general condition that, nonetheless, must be true on the way to the specifics.

10. There are two things going on here. First is the *framing effect*—you interpret the same information differently depending on how it's presented. The second is *loss aversion*—humans are generally more worried about losing x amount than they are excited about gaining the same x amount.

11. Here's another question: which do you find more truthful, the phrase "What sobriety conceals, alcohol reveals," or the phrase "What sobriety conceals, alcohol unmasks"? And now you probably see the punch

line: experiments show that people find rhyming phrases more truthful than the same wisdom that doesn't rhyme. It just rings true! Psychologists call this the *rhyme-is-reason effect.*

62. BIASES, HEURISTICS, AND LOGICAL FALLACIES

1. Scope fallacy—consider the common (albeit misquoted) phrase *all that glitters is not gold,* as in the description of the scope fallacy. Now, if you had to connect is-not or not-gold, which would you connect? With this wording, you can't know if all that glitters is the substance not-gold, or if all that glitters is-not gold. Same with Disraeli—is it "half the cabinet are-not asses," meaning that at least a distinct 50 percent act unlike asses, or is it "half the cabinet are not-asses," in which case it implies that half are? In any case, Plato would agree that it's not much of an *apology.*

2. Ambiguity—Bill Clinton didn't lie … he just didn't tell the truth. In this case the phrase "sexual relations" is ambiguous. Now the whole world knows the comment was, er, fallacious.

3. Guilt by association—this is a type of association fallacy with the formal structure *A is a B; A is also a C; therefore B is a C.* In this and many related cases, *Nazis are bad; Nazis practiced psychiatry; therefore psychiatry is bad.*

4. Appeal to nature—what can be more right than nature? And as a corollary, everything unnatural is bad, including GMO foods and man-made vaccines.

5. Denying the antecedent—Ah, how Turing jests! His example is about as logical as stating that if you're hungry after eight hours, you're human. You're not hungry after eight hours, so you're not human.

6. Tu quoque (You also)—More generally, tu quoque is a form of ad hominem, which is more colloquially described as *I'm right because you suck.* In this case, Osama bin Laden attacks the character of his accuser rather than the content of the argument.

7. False dilemma—In this case, Pawlenty implies the choice must be between his plan and Obama's, when there are certainly other options.

His argument looks like this: Something has to be done; this is something; therefore this has to be done. Not so much.

8. Appeal to authority—if the authority in question is an actual expert with definite facts or opinions, appealing to authority can, in fact, add logical punch to an argument. However, in this case it helps to know that the CBO was frank about its lack of confidence in its own numbers. Bachmann states as fact what the authority took with a grain of salt.

9. Post hoc ergo propter hoc—when one thing comes after or with another, we have the unfortunate predisposition to imagine that the first *caused* the second. Scroll through non-journal science headlines and in the course of a day, you'll find fifty claims of false causation.

10. False dilemma—Only a Sith deals in absolutes, as in Anakin Skywalker's ultimatum to his former teacher Obi-Wan Kenobi: "If you're not with me, then you're my enemy." False dilemma disregards the world's shades of gray.

ACKNOWLEDGMENTS

Thanks to all the scientists who helped me sift through the tangle of conflicting information that is the field of brain research; to my wife, a psychologist, for allowing me to bounce ideas off her trained brain and for offering, without meaning to, an endless source of things to poke fun at in these pages; to my young kids for helping me test cognitive skills of attention, focus, and performance under pressure by periodically and unexpectedly pummeling me with foam light sabers; and to my spectacular agent, Jen, and editor, Julian, for helping to shape this unique resource.